DO YOU DRESS SMART™?
You only have seven seconds to make an impression. Clothes make the difference—dress smart.

1. I work for a traditional law firm with a strict corporate dress code. I am traveling with my boss to a three-day conference, and we leave on a Sunday afternoon. Can I wear my weekend jeans and sneakers on our flight? ....YES or NO

2. Do I need to wear a suit to my interview if I know the office dresses casually? ....YES or NO

3. I don't see my upper management very often, so is there any point in making an investment in my business wardrobe? ....YES or NO

4. I am an accountant at a firm that employs a corporate dress code. I have a meeting at a client's company that has a casual dress code. Should I follow their dress code for the meeting? ....YES or NO

5. I just started work at a corporation where the dress code states women must wear hosiery. I don't know anyone who wears panty hose in the summertime. Do you think it's okay to ignore it? ....YES or NO

6. I am forty years old in a youth-oriented company. I'm in competition for a promotion. Should I update my image with a more fashion forward (i.e. younger) look? ....YES or NO

7. I think my boss dresses too casually for her position. Is it okay for me to dress more formally than she does? ....YES or NO

8. I have a great black minidress that shows off my best feature—long legs. Would it be appropriate to wear to my office Christmas party? ....YES or NO

9. I got a promotion and now oversee an entire department. Since a suit is a suit, whether I pay $ or $$$, do I need to change my wardrobe? ....YES or NO

10. I believe I should be judged by the work I do and not the way I look. Does it really make a difference whether I "dress the part," if my work is good? ....YES or NO

1. no 2. yes 3. yes 4. no 5. no 6. no 7. yes 8. no 9. yes 10. yes

DRESS
SMART™
WOMEN

Wardrobes That Win in the New Workplace

Kim Johnson Gross & Jeff Stone
Text by Kristina Zimbalist
Photos by David Bashaw

WARNER BOOKS

An AOL Time Warner Company

Text by Kristina Zimbalist
Photographs by David Bashaw
Set Stylist Renee Yan
Editorial Consultant Matthew Mol

 An AOL Time Warner Company

Printed in England
First printing: September 2002
10 9 8 7 6 5 4 3 2 1

Library of Congress Catologing-in-Publication Data

Gross, Kim Johnson.
Dress smart--women : wardrobes that win in the new workplace / Kim Johnson Gross &
Jeff Stone ; text by Kristina Zimbalist ; photos by David Bashaw.
p. cm - (Chic simple)
Includes index.
ISBN 0-446-53044-1
1. Clothing and dress. 2. Success in business. I. Stone, Jeff,
1953- II. Zimbalist,
Kristina. III. Title. IV. Series

TT507.G74 2002
660'.2842-dc21

2002066190

Separations by Butler & Tanner Limited

CHIC SIMPLE is a primer for living well but sensibly. It's for those who believe that quality of life comes not from accumulating things but in paring down to the essentials. Chic Simple enables readers to bring value and style into their lives with economy and simplicity.

"It is possible through the skillful manipulation of dress in any particular situation to evoke a favorable response to your positioning and your needs."

JOHN T. MOLLOY
New Dress for Success

Dear Reader,

To paraphrase John T. Molloy—people do judge a book by its cover. Right or wrong, it's the real world. Dressing appropriately in today's workplace is essential. Your clothes are the first impression you make whether on a job interview, representing your firm to a new client, or making a presentation within your company. Bottom line: You should always dress for the job you want, and for your professional goals.

But today the simple act of dressing can be confusing. Mistakes can be costly not only to your budget, but to your career. *Dress Smart*™ offers practical guidelines and sound, simple advice to help you determine your best professional wardrobe.

This book has been culled from our own experience as consultants, but in these pages we also share the personal experiences and advice of successful women in a variety of industries who discuss the importance clothes have had in their careers. And throughout *Dress Smart*™ we answer questions we receive daily on the Chic

Simple web site (www.chicsimple.com) from women around the country who are plagued with real work wear questions.

We feel that the two *Dress Smart*™ books (we've also written a companion to this book, *Dress Smart*™ *Men*) are the most important of the 25 Chic Simple titles we have published over the last 10 years. Why? Because *Dress Smart*™ will give you the confidence that accompanies dressing appropriately and with authority. Whether you want to get a job, be a success at your present job, or get a better job—*Dress Smart*™ is the first crucial step because small investments in your wardrobe lead to large payoffs in your career. Don't hesitate to invest in yourself.

Now go get dressed.

Kim and jeff

"The more you know, the less you need."
AUSTRALIAN ABORIGINAL SAYING

HOW TO use this book

It's broken into the three major aspects of your work life/career:

1. GET JOB (hard to work without one)
2. SUCCEED IN JOB (good idea)
3. GET BETTER JOB (better is better)

At each stage, *Dress Smart*™ reviews the issues you should be aware of, concrete ways to convert the ideas into clothes, and examples of how to work those clothes into everyday life. We use the **image guides** to do the translating; each critical stage ends with a sample closet.

1. GET JOB. If you are leaving college and going out into the job market, if you are reentering the job market after a mommy track interval, or maybe you just decided to get serious about the whole job/career thing and want to shoot for something different, this is the section for you. The principles are the same no matter which circumstance describes you.

2. SUCCEED IN JOB. You've decided that work is a significant part of your life. You are serious about taking it to the next stage and you want never to worry about whether you look appropriate or not. No matter the moment or opportunity, your clothes should be a secret asset.

3. GET BETTER JOB. Great, you did it, achieved a major position. Now what? For years, men have dressed for leadership, from military uniforms to power suits. Now it's your turn. You go, girl, and *Dress Smart*™ will show you how. It's easy: Turn the pages, read, look, and think about what you want your clothes to say about you.

1 GET JOB

SUCCEED IN JOB 2

3

GET BETTER JOB

GOES WITH THE JOB

4

SEXPOT SEEKING SUITABLE POSITION

Dear Kim and jeff,
I am interviewing for an advertising position and am considering wearing
a more modern outfit than a traditional suit. Because it is advertising, I
want to show some spunk and creativity. My suit is black, and I wear an
ivory blouse and two-inch pumps with it. Instead, I am considering a
black silk suit with pinstripes, a very short skirt, a lace camisole, textured
black hose, and black three-inch sling backs. Any thoughts?
—Sling Back Curious

Dear Sling Back Curious,
Creativity doesn't mean sexy. A very short skirt, lacy camisole, textured
hose, and three-inch sling backs will get in the way of your message. A male
interviewer may be uncomfortable with your appearance, and a female
may be annoyed. To show your individuality, wear your black suit and add
a decorative pin, necklace, or scarf, or replace the ivory shirt with one in an
interesting print. The sling backs will work with nude or sheer black
hosiery. The goal is to look professional, not like you're going on a date.

—Kim and jeff

Get Job 1

Interview Wardrobe

1–2–3–4–5–6–7. That's the amount of time it takes for someone to decide your career path. After just seven seconds, a person makes an impression: Competent or a Disaster. Pulled Together or a Flake. Confident or Wilting Violet. A Credit to My Hiring Skills or What an Embarrassment. Which side of the dichotomy do you want to land on? How can you ensure that during those critical first seconds you come across as strong as possible? Give yourself a chance. Dress to get the job. Dress smart.

1. Get Job

If You're So Smart, Why Do You Dress So Stupid?
—Clothes and Career

> "No matter how talented you are or how hard you try, if you don't know the rules you don't succeed."
>
> **JOHN GRAY**
> *Mars and Venus in the Workplace*

Twelve years into her tenure as *Today* show coanchor, Katie Couric was informed, along with the rest of the nation, that the coiffed and sophisticated Diane Sawyer would be cohosting a similar morning show, one network—a click of the remote control—away. Immediately following the announcement, Couric's every-girl image underwent a series of not-so-subtle changes. Her run-of-the-mill pants were replaced with trendy plaid skirts. Plain pumps made way for ultrapointy stilettos. Dowdy cardigans were tossed in favor of sorbet-colored cashmere sweaters, and high-style blazers were paired with crisp white shirts. Her mousy brown hair turned seven shades of blond, her pixie boy cut became a flirty flip, and her mouth morphed into a glossy pout. In a matter of weeks, all signs of news anchor stuffiness had been banished to the post-10 A.M. hour.

Grilling heads of state, four-star chefs, and celebrities hardly requires glamour clothes. After all, the tried-and-true anonymous suit took Barbara Walters, Jane Pauley, and crew to the top of their fields. But when the competition turned fierce, Couric realized, every detail would make a difference. And the woman who had once scoffed at style segments, almost wincing as she mocked the word "fee-ashion," realized she could no longer afford to consider a polished appearance a frivolous trifle. It had become a job requirement.

REALITY CHECK
The way you dress makes a difference in the way you work. When your image signals success, your success potential increases.

CHANGE YOUR IMAGE, CHANGE YOUR LIFE

Most working women won't find themselves battling a talented rival a few channels away. But what about a few cubicles away? When the economy took a plunge early in the new millennium, thousands of the nation's workers were laid off, unemployment skyrocketed, and each available job had seemingly infinite applicants vying for it. The result: Advantage went to the employers, who could afford to hire the person who ranked highest in every category on the job requirement list, and even a few that didn't. One check against you—whether it was a typo on your résumé or a suede jacket worn to an interview at a strictly corporate company—could be a deal breaker.

Whether you like it or not—no matter what the state of the economy—the way you present yourself from your suit cut and hair length to your heel height and style of handbag acts as a thumbnail sketch of your character, subject to instant interpretation by those around you. From these visual cues, others make assumptions about your dedication and competence; your personality, habits, tastes; social life, friends, and quirks. The thought and effort you put into determining what you wear will directly correlate to the strength, accuracy, and consistency of the message you give out.

Faced with the reality that her clothes would have an impact on her career, Katie Couric took control of her wardrobe, and, instead of mocking it, made it work for her. It's a decision every working woman must consider if she intends to get what she wants from her career.

THE POWER OF IMAGE

We live in a visual society. Presidents recognize the importance of being camera-savvy. Celebrities hire stylists to ensure their clothes send just the right message. And companies spend billions of dollars to project an image that has impact by dressing their product up in ideas and symbols they want to claim as their own. When Pepsi splashed Britney Spears across its ads, the brand became instantly young and hip by association, suggesting that the time-tested classic was also part of the MTV generation. Ralph Lauren consistently shoots his ad campaigns in sprawling country homes and equestrian settings, and so his name has become synonymous with American prosperity and heritage.

At work, you are the brand. And your look is your logo—it should

1. Get Job

THE RIGHT TO ADORN
You have every right to decorate your body as you see fit. However, do you represent the type of employee your interviewer is looking for? That's the question. Your freedom to have piercings and tattoos is guaranteed. Your right to have a particular job, however, is in the eye of the beholder (the beholder of the job that is being offered). If expressing who you are through these adornments is important to you, then you also have the right to not take the job. If the opportunity the job offers is worth some self-adjustment, well, it's your call.

send a clear, consistent message about who you are, what you have to offer, where you want to go. Your task is to pinpoint the identity you want to have within your working environment and then dress to express it. If you don't, you're leaving your identity—or influential others' impression of it, at least—up to fate and chance. Decide to put the effort into choosing clothes that reflect who you are, and you take control of your career and your life.

CLOTHES AS BRAND ATTRIBUTES

During the first 25 years of her career, megalawyer Gloria Allred was rarely spotted wearing anything but a bright red power suit. "TV loves red. My name is 'all-red.' It just ended up being my thing. I became known for it. And because it was consistent and unique to me, it helped me make a statement."

Business is big on visual cues. Red = power. Pinstripes = authority. A crisp white shirt shows you can roll up your sleeves and get down to business. A briefcase signals utter efficiency. On the other hand, clothes that are rumpled or a handbag that is oversized and crammed scream unpreparedness and irresponsibility, whether it's true or not. Studies show that presentation can even influence, if unconsciously, the perceived quality of one's work: A go-getter assistant who's always wearing a tailored suit will be thought of one way (highly promotable); an equally ambitious woman who wears baggy khakis and V-neck sweaters might be thought of in another (a chronic support staffer). Your clothes can even reveal whether you're detail oriented or not (polish those shoes!).

What are your work clothes saying about you? A collared shirt: "Yes ma'am." A sharp suit: "I'm ready for action." A tattoo: "Make me."

DRESSING SMART

This is what "dressing smart" is not: A fleeting fad. The latest stiletto. Androgynous exec-dressing. An uptight uniform. This is what it is: Finding a consistent, predominantly classic style that works for your personality, your office environment, and the career path you want to take. As your career progresses, you will develop a personal style that reveals aspects of your personality and status. The goal at this stage is to wear clothes that give you office cred—that are appropriate to your environment, and convey a sense of professionalism, polish, and credibility.

> "I have always felt that you should be able to throw a magazine on the floor at any page and know whose magazine it is."
>
> **TINA BROWN**
> Founder, *Talk* magazine

DRESSING (SMART) FOR SUCCESS

The career-boosting power of clothes is hardly a new notion. In 1961, John T. Molloy published the groundbreaking book *Dress for Success*, with the subtitle: *Dress Like a Million So You Can Make a Million*. He was the first to even broach the notion that the mere way they dressed could make executives more effective, lawyers win cases, salesmen see skyrocketing sales, and any employee attain a speedier promotion and bigger pay raise.

For decades, the "dress for success" logic was a fact of business life. Then suddenly the pendulum swung and the last decade witnessed the dressed up backlash: Dot-commers ushered in an era where khakis were a career move (just spruce up your portfolio, and you had it made). The rise of the Britney Spears generation and the burgeoning Gen Y demographic saw bright young rebels suddenly considered a business asset—which brought bare midriffs and pierced navels into the offices of publishing houses and PR firms.

Today, work is once again serious business. And everyone is expected to look it. This book will help you determine what that means for your career and your goals. It's not just Katie Couric who gets ratings. In this economy, it's always sweeps month. And your clothes better measure up.

GET JOB

The first step is to get a job. In the current economy, this can present a challenge—every detail is critical. The main objective: Dress the part. Call human resources to find out the dress code. Research the company, and show up wearing clothes that reflect its values, ethic, and style. This is not a time to make fashion statements. The way you present yourself is an instant synopsis to your future employer of your professionalism, dedication, reliability, and character. It's important to put your best foot forward.

SUCCEED IN JOB

Every industry has its jargon—subtleties of speech that separate the insiders from the wanna-bes. The same slang exists in the dress code.

Once you have the job, the emphasis turns to filling your closet with appropriate, lasting clothes that will serve you in every situation the job presents: A TV producer might discover that black denim worn

1. Get Job

with a blazer strikes a suitably hip yet still authoritative note. A Wall Street trader might realize that, while a suit is not required, it sharpens her image and increases her credibility when meeting with clients. Think about the message you want to send and how to say it best. Part of clarifying your message will mean getting rid of items that confuse it, whether it's the headband you've worn since college or the preppy blazer that went with it.

GET BETTER JOB

How does your boss dress? Once you have the industry lingo down, the goal is to sharpen and strengthen your look so that it does some of the work to get you to your next position. An assistant might find that starting to wear a suit makes higher-ups view her in a more responsible and independent light. The Wall Street exec might decide that carrying a fashionable handbag shows her clients that she's both successful and up on current trends. Again, at this stage, it's important to assess details: Does the denim you wear on Fridays undermine the authority you establish during the week? Are your suits and shoes in excellent condition and of a quality that's up to par with a higher position? Settle on a refined color palette and personalized accessories that further define you and your work style.

DRESS SMART—EVERY DAY

Wearing clothes that actively serve you is an ongoing process. Styles change. Your age changes. Your body might change. You might enter a new industry. It's important to make periodic assessments and be aware of the subtle shifts in dress codes and visual communications at all times. Every so often, take a truly objective look at your closet, and in the mirror, and make sure your work clothes are appropriate, effective, and working as hard as you do.

How to Dress Smart™
—The Chic Simple Process

ASSESS, DEJUNK, RENEW—THE PROCESS

The Chic Simple Process is about achieving simplicity in any area of
your life—from your photo albums to your finances—by following
three steps: 1. Assess: Setting aside time to think about your lifestyle
needs and your aesthetic preferences; 2. DeJunk: Discovering what you
have outgrown (and can get rid of), and what you are missing; and
3. ReNew: Filling in the blanks with items more purely in synch with
your current goals and state of mind. It's that simple.

1. Assess
Assess and survey. Take account of how you live your life
and what you own. These are the key two areas of examination you need to engage in. Match your possessions
with your life and voilà—your focus returns.

A PROCESS OF SIMPLICITY

2. DeJunk
DeJunk and recycle. Simplify is a verb, a practice. You
must act, deal with all that is superfluous, think hard
about what you actually need, edit ruthlessly. In the end, it
will save you grief, time, and money.

3. ReNew
ReNew and replace. You thought about what you need,
you got rid of what you didn't need, and now it's time to
fill in the holes. Does this mean shopping or rethinking?
Learn how you can prevent repeating mistakes.

1. Get Job

1. ASSESS: YOUR INTERVIEW WARDROBE

Unless you're a Hollywood production assistant or a first-year lawyer, your early career isn't likely to dominate your life. So it's understandable that your early work wardrobe shares space with your lifelong play clothes. First step: Separate the two—work clothes from play clothes, sneakers from pumps (production assistants, again, please ignore) so you have a clear view, from now on, of your business options. Organize the items in your closet as methodically as you do your Rolodex™, so they're as easy to access as your phone numbers. Put blouses together, shoes together, suits together. Find a place for scarves. You wouldn't toss papers into your desk drawer à la Hurricane Hugo, would you? Treat your shoes with the same efficiency. If you don't own shoe trees, buy some.

Work clothes require special upkeep, scrutiny, dedication, and strategy. Begin considering them with the same ambition and organization as you do your work.

2. DEJUNK: CLOSET INVENTORY

Now that you can see into your closet, what do you have? Get rid of anything you haven't worn in the last year—if you haven't worn it in the last twelve months, chances are you won't wear it next year. If you have suits that don't fit, take them to the tailor. If you have shoes that are appallingly scuffed (or rain-warped or otherwise disfigured), take them to the shoe repairman or save them for rainy-day commutes. And finally, get rid of anything that is so small, obsolete, or simply unattractive (don't be embarrassed, tastes change) that you wouldn't wear it to the office tomorrow.

3. RENEW: SHOPPING YOUR CLOSET

Take a critical look at what's left. The key question: What's missing? Do you have suits but not enough accessories? Are you swarming with scarves but have only one good pair of shoes? Make a list of everything you have in your closet in one column; in the next column, write what you would need to utilize those items to their full potential (left: skirt. right: sweater set, pearls, sling backs, nude hosiery). The right-hand column is an ongoing shopping list that you should carry with you in case you're ever in a store and wondering what you need (impulse buys, begone!). Circle the items that could go with more

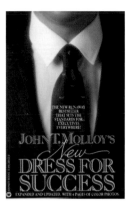

**THANK YOU,
JOHN MOLLOY**
The important feature of Molloy's book was his exercises for testing his theories about clothes and how people would react to them. He would test everyone, from receptionists to doormen to maitre d's by having people try to deliver parcels to executives, get into a doorman building, or acquire a table at a restaurant. By recruiting variously dressed individuals in different outfits and color combinations he was able to deduce the power of suits, raincoats, and shirt and tie combinations—which proved that appearances count, especially to receptionists.

than one thing in your closet. When you go to the store, buy these items first—because of their versatility, they make the smartest buys and best bargains.

SHOP SMART, WEAR EVERYTHING
Shop for your closet the way a pro plays a hand of gin: Pick up a new item only if it completes a look, or if you already own at least two items that will go with it. The goal is to fill your closet with functional clothes where you wear every single item you own.

ARE YOU DRESSING FOR YOUR GOALS?
Below are six questions to ask yourself about your wardrobe; but before you do, get out a pad and pen. Why? Because any consultant, financial planner, self-discovery workshop, or personal trainer will tell you progress is made only by writing down your goals and then referring back to them.

1. Are all your clothes versatile and do they work well together?
2. Do you have a basic neutral palette as a core to your wardrobe?
3. No lies—does everything fit or should some things be altered (or DeJunked)?
4. Do you have a yearly budget for your career wardrobe?
5. Do you own a minimum of four suits to work your wardrobe around?
6. Do all your work clothes make you feel and look comfortable and confident?

Cracking the Three Dress Codes

—What to Wear to the Job Interview

CORPORATE
When corporate attire means a pantsuit, pumps, and high quality leather, accessories pack professional punch.

DRESS CODES OF BUSINESS

"When I was 22, I was a network executive at CBS," says Jane Rosenthal, a producer and partner (with Robert De Niro) in Tribeca Films. "So here I was, this kid, at the time the youngest ranking female network exec, and I was constantly trying to figure out the style. People who walked into my office would always have an impact on me—I would try to absorb what they were wearing. I wore conservative suits because I felt like I had to. I wore respectable pumps. Then inevitably I would show up wearing something like red nail polish and notice a lot of people staring at my red hands as I spoke. That was my method for realizing when there was something I probably shouldn't wear."

A dress code is a slippery slope. There are rarely hard and fast rules. And the lines between corporate and casual are constantly shifting. The task of navigating such sartorial subtleties might seem a daunting prospect. But basically there are three main modes of business dress, one of which your workplace will likely fall into.

THE CORPORATE DRESS CODE

In a corporate environment—a law firm, a financial institution—the suit is the standard uniform. Women, like their male colleagues, generally are expected to wear a suit. A sweater and skirt or blouse and skirt can be appropriate at one's desk, as long as a jacket is within snagging

BUSINESS APPROPRIATE
Pulled together but a tad relaxed, this look calls for a comfortably clean handbag and shoes.

CASUAL
When the suit teams up with a T-shirt and sneakers, the look is authority with attitude.

distance to be tossed on at a moment's notice. Acceptable suit undergarments include a blouse, a crisp shirt, or a knit sweater or shell. Other guidelines for the sartorially strict office: Legs must always be covered by stockings. Shoes should be closed-toe with a low to medium heel.

THE BUSINESS APPROPRIATE DRESS CODE

The business-appropriate world is halfway between corporate and casual. In this world, a suit is not obligatory, but the idea is to choose clothes that approximate its polish and decorum: A skirt and blouse or sweater set worn with heels or boots; tailored trousers paired with a turtleneck and jacket.

THE BUSINESS CASUAL DRESS CODE

The motto of business casual: No jacket required. This most laid-back dress code is the one many corporate offices adopted for Fridays (sending thousands of choice-addled lawyers and investment bankers fleeing to "I'm Lost without My Suit" seminars, desperately seeking fashion solace). Despite assumptions to the contrary, a casual dress code does not mean fashion anarchy. In fact, the more lax the look, the more important it is to abide by certain rules: Clothes must be pressed and immaculately presentable. Mix a casual item with something more traditionally businesslike—ironed khakis with a classic white shirt; a casual skirt and a sweater set; a clean, tailored pair of dark jeans (in certain offices only) with a jacket. No tank tops. No concert T-shirts. Clothes that are too short, too tight, too sheer, or too low-cut are still unprofessional, even here. A sense of propriety must be maintained at all times.

DRESS CODE EXCEPTIONS

Few careers take place within the confines of four walls. Situations will arise that require a deviation from your standard dress code. And even sartorial pros are called upon to make difficult judgment calls: "Recently I went to a meeting wearing a suede jacket, a cashmere sweater, and a pair of pants," says Nancy Novogrod, fashion-savvy editor in chief of *Travel & Leisure* magazine. "It was with a cable TV company and I figured everyone would be dressed down. But I was surprised, they really weren't. I was underdressed and that was embarrassing."

1. Get Job

Other professionals are dress-code swingers. One film executive was on set with her director and crew on the coldest day of the year. She wore jeans, long underwear, leather and lambskin boots with heaters in them, and layers of North Face and Patagonia. The next week, she was at a finance meeting for the next film, dressed in leather pants and a blazer.

> "I have yet to hear a man ask for advice on how to combine marriage and a career."
>
> **GLORIA STEINEM**
> Founder, *MS* magazine

YOUR DRESS CODE

Every office has its clothes quirks and unwritten rules—jeans must be dressed up with a jacket; suits are mandatory at meetings; ankle length skirts are unprofessional. When you pay attention, the intricacies of this inside information will become apparent to you.

No matter which corporate dress code applies, in time you will learn to interpret it in a way that reflects your personality, position, and goals. If you work in a corporate environment: Are you the pin-stripe type? Do you have a weakness for pale pink or a passion for power red? Developing a personal business style is a lifelong process. The further up the ladder you go, the more freedom you have to inject your personal tastes. Until then, and whenever you're in doubt, stick with the classics.

RESEARCHING INDUSTRY DRESS CODES

Determining what you will be expected to wear requires research. First, familiarize yourself with the boundaries of the firm you are interviewing with. Look at their web site, then place a call to the company's human resources department to fine-tune the office specifics. The chaos of a new office presents enough unknowns—feeling comfortable with the basic clothing requirements will give you instant confidence and security.

TARGET AUDIENCE—PRESENTING YOURSELF

When composing your visual sound bite, it's crucial that you take into account who's listening.

"Colorado is casual," says former congresswoman Pat Schroeder. "So when I was campaigning, I usually wore dresses, sometimes a shirt and skirt. In fact, if you showed up wearing a suit they'd probably think you were the concierge at the hotel." However, if Hillary Clinton, while running for the Senate in New York, hadn't worn a suit, her potential constituents would have concluded that she didn't take the job seriously.

A news editor working behind a desk at the *New York Times* might be adequately outfitted in khakis and a sweater. A head buyer at Barneys New York, a public relations representative, or the CEO of eBay would not.

Be aware of your audience, your surroundings, and the unspoken subtleties that aren't listed in the dress code. Killer stilettos might be red hot at MTV, but result in a pink slip for a banker.

MONEY IN THE BANK
If you won't invest in yourself, why would someone else?

MY INTERVIEW INVESTMENT
You are about to invest in yourself to get the job you want. Reality check: It takes money to make money. What is this job worth to you? Take into account where you are in your career path. What makes for a sensible investment for a first job is very different from what is required for a crucial key position later in life. For now, Assess. Determine what you need and what you can afford. Fill out the form below (with your best guesses as to costs) and then sign off on it. This is your commitment to yourself.

I need to purchase a (what color)_____ suit to better present myself in a job interview. To complete my interview outfit I also need (how many)_____ tops, a pair of black shoes, black leather purse, (how many) _____ pairs of hose. I estimate these items will cost the following:

Suit	_____	Purse	_____
Top	_____	Shoes	_____
Top	_____	Hose	_____
Top	_____	Other	_____
Top	_____	Total	_____

In the first year of my career I will make (approximate first-year salary) $ _____ ; minus what I will spend on clothes (wardrobe investment) $ _____ equals $ _____ . This is my ROI (RETURN ON INVESTMENT).

Your Name_____
Congratulations, now go shop.

industry guidelines

There are no *Cliff's Notes* deciphering the subtleties and symbolism that lie hidden within industry dress codes. We've done some fieldwork—interviewing professionals and human resources managers in various fields—to determine the guidelines that tend to remain consistent within each particular profession. Bottom line: Dress conservatively while interviewing, and, once you get the job, be alert. Each office has a distinct culture and a fashion slang with it.

Who Wears What To Work

Deciphering Industry Dress Codes

ACADEMIC

"It's very tweedy, very preppy. I know academia from all sides," says Carol Gill, a former admissions officer who went on to head her own college guidance firm. Whether the job is dean of students or tenured professor, the academic dress code is the same: Business casual. That means tailored, presentable pieces that are authoritative but still approachable. Geography and, at times, the nature of the school will determine the exact interpretation. A Columbia biology professor situated in uptown New York City is likely to dress differently from her counterpart at the New Hampshire–based Dartmouth. Either way, the message is the same: "I dress to inspire confidence," Gill says. "To let people know I'm a professional who hasn't just come on the scene."

CONSULTING

A consultant should dress to establish herself as a figure of authority with the company for whom she's consulting. Generally, this means a suit. Dressing professionally can serve another key purpose for those giving advice: It helps ensure they'll look worthy of the money the company is shelling out for the outside expertise.

RETAIL

Retail and manufacturing executive Joanne Langer is the CEO of the clothes manufacturer Garfield & Marks, a corporation that also owns fashion labels, including Tahari. "I wear everything from a suit to a sweater and slacks," she says. "If I need to be incredibly presidential, I wear a power suit. If I'm discussing a strategy and want everyone to be part of it, I dress more approachably in a sweater and slacks."

A retail salesperson's appearance should represent the merchandise she is selling and the caliber of her clientele. Someone selling khakis at the Gap will dress differently from her counterpart in designer sportswear at Saks. "Appearance contributes to the response in whomever you're trying to communicate with," Langer says. "If a salesperson is saying, 'This suit is classic and beautiful,' and she has blue hair and a nose ring, the customer thinks, 'How would you know?'"

SERVICE INDUSTRY

Service positions—hotel managers, restaurant workers—often require a uniform. Otherwise, the rule of thumb is to wear crisp, well-ironed, and presentable clothes that fall into the business casual or business appropriate range, depending on the position.

ADVERTISING

Like many creative media, the dress code in advertising tends to be corporate creative. For entry-level positions, that means whatever is in fashion at the moment—low-rider pants or ladylike dresses. "Because it's a creative environment, it's more acceptable than it would be at a Fortune 500 company," says Beth Silver, vice president/director of HR at Grey Advertising. Midlevel employees take liberties within a corporate casual to business appropriate range: "You see the Ann Taylor look; I've also seen a lot of leather and a purple suede shirt worn with three or four long gold necklaces," she says. Senior executives dress with similar diversity, in everything from high fashion Armani to devil-may-care denim. Clearly, the more conservative the firm—or a particular client—the more conservative the dress.

FINANCIAL

While skirt suits, stockings, and high heels were once the norm, investment banking and its financial counterparts have slightly loosened their dress demands in recent years. "A pantsuit is fine," says Aimee Brown, formerly of Goldman Sachs and founding partner of Artemis Capital, Inc. Investment bankers and financiers like to present an image of power and also monetary success to their clients, and so a business appropriate look is key. In New York suits or a look approximating it is common. But location is everything. Brown went on to start her own investment firm in San Francisco, where "slacks and a jacket and a sweater or a blouse is common. Nobody seems to be wearing hose. You can wear flats or heels. You do see some skirts around, but not a formal business skirt. If someone has a meeting, the look will be more suitlike. But in general, people wear a more casual look."

MEDICINE

"Some of the policies describe the medical dress code as 'tasteful and professional,'" Pam Tarulli, assistant director of HR at Lenox Hill Hospital and Manhattan Eye, Ear, and Throat Hospital. "What it means is no low-cut blouses, no spandex, no short skirts that rise so far above the knee—and yes, we give an actual number measurement." As a dermatologist with an independent practice, Francesca Fusco can dress any way she chooses, and she's most comfortable with a philosophy similar to Tarulli's. "People are coming to you as an authority, and you have to look the part," Fusco says. "I don't wear a lot of jewelry. I keep my nails moderately short, with a French manicure—nothing bright, nothing red. And I like to wear a white coat at all times. Underneath it, I'll wear suits or pants or a dress. But if I'm wearing an outfit that would look good with high suede boots, I'll wear them." And while laws prevent companies from discriminating based on appearance, those who work for larger companies must be careful with the liberties they take. "At one hospital we had a woman with vibrant neon hair. She was the best phlebotomist [drawer of blood] we had, but people got afraid of that, especially the elderly."

LAW

"Until recently, I didn't believe in wearing pants to the DA's office, and certainly not to court," says Linda Fairstein, head of sex crimes in the district attorney's office in New York. "I didn't think it looked professional." While law and banking are considered the last bastions of truly formal business attire, even their staunch guidelines have softened in recent years. In metropolitan regions, a suit is compulsory, though pants are now commonplace, and closed-toe shoes and stockinged legs are required. These and other particulars—including skirt length, Friday dress, courtroom attire—are governed by the mandates of each individual firm. In smaller towns, lawyerly dress codes are determined on a case by case basis. "I've worn leather pants to court, though not in front of a jury," says Rhode Island attorney Lise Gescheidt. "Beach communities are much more casual. Lawyers don't wear socks in the summer, people show up with wet hair. You have to play to your audience. If you're too polished, people could perceive you as pandering or condescending. That doesn't advance the ball."

MEDIA

Jobs in the media—television and film production, magazine publishing—generally inspire a creative take on business attire. Translation: Suits with an edge. "Hollywood is such a boys' club," says producer Jane Rosenthal, former executive at CBS and partner in Robert De Niro's Tribeca Films. "On one hand, I wanted to be respectful of the people who came in to sell projects to me—which meant a suit—but there was always something a little off. I'd wear it with lace, or pearls and leather. It's a creative community. If you dressed 100% normal, they'd look at you a bit odd." Most media jobs hearken to this philosophy: Associate producers on down wear business appropriate attire, often with a hip twist (special note to production assistants and others who do glamorous grunt work: denim and Dockers are de rigueur).

The further up the corporate ladder one travels, however, the less "creative" the dress code. Paramount CEO Sherri Lansing, for example, takes her business suits sans leather and lace.

One notable exception: The editor in chief of a magazine, who is almost expected to take a foray into fashion. Editors and assistants tend to follow suit. The magazine dress code tends to be business casual to business appropriate attire, often with a streak of high style.

It's rare for high style to wander into the hallowed halls of book editors, where the common dress is business casual to business appropriate. The marketing side of book publishing thrives on timeliness and trends, and stylish, business appropriate attire is a common uniform.

REAL ESTATE

Manhattan real estate agent Susan Penzer wears the same thing all successful women in her profession wear: Clothes that enable her clients to relate to her. "I'll wear leather pants, a Paul Smith denim blazer, Ted Muehling earrings, good handbags. I have a lot of fashion clients, directors, and photographers—they feel I look like them so they can connect with me." But as they say, location is everything. In contrast, a real estate agent working in a suburb of Chicago might wear a colorful suit, gold jewelry, and conservative heels.

PUBLIC RELATIONS

"Some companies come to a PR firm to find creativity and edge," says Liz Kaplow, president of the Manhattan-based Kaplow Communications. "We have to satisfy those expectations down to our clothes." For Kaplow that means suits with a dash of fashion. For those in nonexecutive PR positions, even more fashion freedom is allowed. No matter what level the employee, however, one rule always applies: The nature of the client can sway the dress code. "If you're with a very corporate client," Kaplow says, "know enough to streamline your look and be a little bit more conservative."

ARCHITECTURE

The dress code in architecture is similar to that in advertising. "No jeans, no sneakers, no T-shirts. Casual but neat," says Nina Bransfield, marketing manager at the SoHo firm Fox & Fowle. And, more often than not, creative. "But when you go to any kind of client meeting, the dress is business attire." Translation: Suits. As with any industry, larger, more formal firms can often have more conservative dress codes.

ACCOUNTING

"I personally wear a suit four days out of five," says Manhattan accounting executive Sandra Kaufman. "I haven't always, but we're in a position of giving advice, and I find that you get more respect when you dress appropriately." Generally, those in executive accounting positions tend to dress in corporate attire. But for all other accounting titles—bookkeepers, semisenior accountants, assistants—"it's a lot more casual," Kaufman says. Smaller accounting firms may be corporate casual while larger firms often require their paraprofessionals to dress professionally, aka business appropriate.

INTERNET

"The Internet has evolved into just another medium, and the dress code is media dress," says Maya Draisin, founder of the International Academy of Digital Arts and Sciences, and executive with the Webby Awards, the Oscars of the Internet. "The styles are slightly edgier, there is more individuality." While anything-goes is still the rule at dot-coms, slacker khakis have begun to be traded in for cutting-edge fashion and the latest techno looks. "You see heels, but they're not conservative pumps—it's a thicker heel, an interesting toe," Draisin says. "One woman showed up for an interview in a traditional suit and I almost didn't hire her, it was such a shock to my system."

Dress Better, Spend Less
—Wardrobe Economics

POWER OF THREE
For maximum value and versatility, buy a suit jacket along with its matching pants and skirt.

DRESSING FOR THE JOB INTERVIEW

An Energizer bunny work ethic doesn't come across in an interview. A tailored suit, neat hair, and polished shoes do.

You've slaved to get a college degree, polished your skills, and networked like crazy. An appearance that's less than stellar can sabotage all of that. The subliminal power of a visual cue is a psychological fact. One that, as we've discussed, leads marketers to spend billions. You need to represent your product—your ability and professionalism—on the outside. Unlike the mind-blowing qualifications that fill your résumé, your appearance is the element that is in everyone's face, every day. Other candidates are giving their wardrobe a high level of attention. You can't afford not to.

INVEST IN YOURSELF

Dressing up to your potential costs money. Your initial wardrobe will cost more than your prom dress, less than your wedding dress. But the payoff, thankfully, will be much closer to the latter than the former. You're investing in your confidence, value, packaging. You're showing people what you have on the inside. It's the unspoken cue that relays your capability and worthiness all day, every day. A cheap suit will leave you insecure, worried, inferior. A good suit, tailored to fit perfectly, with the right shoes and bag, will make you feel confident,

1. Get Job

appropriate, and raring to go. You're paying for conviction and poise, comfort, self-esteem. You're paying for the luxury of forgetting what you're wearing so you can get on with the job at hand.

CLOTHES COST. REALISTIC EXPECTATIONS

Once sold on appearance power, pure ambition might lead you to head straight to the Armani racks. Then reality sets in. It's the time in your life when you have the least amount of money, and you want to make the best impression. An equally stunning, suitably professional look can be attained on a much more realistic budget. You need to know how and what to buy—where to put the money, and where it's okay to skimp.

SHOP SMART. QUALITY = VALUE

The goal when shopping for a smart wardrobe is to keep the wallet outlay at a minimum, while keeping one key factor in mind: The better the quality of the item you buy, the better it will make you look, and the longer it will last.

"When I first started out, in my 20s, I would go to thrift shops and consignment stores and buy elegant suits for twenty dollars," says publisher Judith Regan. "They'd be a year old that some rich woman had worn once and had gotten sick of or a designer who had had a surplus. Really nice quality fabric. I'd be really well dressed—but on a budget."

The first step in buying high quality that's affordable is to browse the designer floors. Assess the fit, fabric, quality, and style of the clothes you find there. How are the Armani suits cut? What fabrics does Ralph Lauren use? Try on a Calvin Klein pantsuit to see how they fit. Once you're familiar with the details that denote quality, head to the more affordable racks and look for the closest approximation to those qualities that you can find.

WARDROBE ECONOMICS—ROI (RETURN ON INVESTMENT)

Dressing for less means carefully determining what you are going to spend the most money on. Rule of thumb: Buy items that are classic—not trendy—and good enough that you'll have them forever.

Reserve the largest chunk of your budget for your suit. It must be a nice fabric—a wool or wool blend is timeless, lasts year round, and is versatile. Choose one with clean, classic lines and in a neutral color (black is most versatile) that will easily mix with other items in your wardrobe. Remember to factor in the cost for tailoring. The items you wear with it—your handbag, your shoes, for example—can be more affordable. After all, under her tuxedo, Sharon Stone wore a Gap T-shirt to the Oscars and drew raves!

SHOP WITH A PLAN

- Dress appropriately.
- Arrive at the store with a well-thought-out list of the items you need.
- Your first purchase should be a versatile suit. All other purchases must go with this core suit.
- Shopping smart takes time and effort. Don't leave it until your lunch hour or the day before the interview. It might take several days of looking and a trip to the tailor for alterations.
- Before you buy any item, make sure it is classic, versatile, fits well, and is flattering to your body type. The color and style should be appropriate for the workplace (no neon; no miniskirts) and compatible with the rest of your professional wardrobe. The fabric and workmanship should be of good quality.
- Don't buy anything without trying it on first.
- If a garment fits but is not your normal size, don't despair: Sizes often differ from brand to brand.

"In preparing for battle I have always found that plans are useless, but planning is indispensable."

DWIGHT D. EISENHOWER

1. Get Job

Now What Are You Going to Buy?
—Shopping for the Interview Outfit

THANK YOU AGAIN, JOHN MOLLOY
Men who wore white shirts were thought to be more competent and honest…
Dress for Success, 1976
(Men in white shirts) were thought to be more intelligent, honest, successful, and powerful than men wearing any other color.
Dress for Success, 1988

THE INTERVIEW WARDROBE—TOOLS TO SUCCESS

When you meet your interviewer for the first time, what impression do you want to give? If you want to say, I'm pretty, wear your favorite frilly blouse. If you want to say, I'm laid-back, wear the V-neck sweater you loved in college. If you want to say, I'm more competent, reliable, and professional than any candidate you will interview for this position—in other words, if you want the job—step one is: Invest in a suit.

Sharp lines and authoritative stance—a suit says power, reliability, independence. And it can make you feel as confident as you look. Your interview suit—and everything that goes with it—is the first tool on your road to success. Settling on the right one can be difficult. The mission: To prepare you to buy an interview suit and the business gear to go with it.

WHAT IS AN INTERVIEW SUIT?

Whether you are just starting out or a CEO looking to switch companies, your interview suit must convey a confident, competent "I've got it together" sense of authority. This is best accomplished with a dark, monochromatic tone (avoid patterns) and a classic cut. That means clean, simple lines around which you will build your entire business wardrobe. Looking sharp doesn't stop once the interview is over—there is always someone further up the food chain, which means there is always someone for whom you need to look smart.

shop smart

Call it the little suit that could. Your interview suit will act as the foundation of your business wardrobe, and you will wear it constantly. This chapter gets down to the nitty-gritty of choosing it well: How a tailored shape and good fabric convey competence; how a neutral color translates to flexibility; how taking your time, choosing a classic shape, and then having it properly tailored provide the best guarantee that you have spent your money well.

How to Buy an Interview Outfit

BEST BUY: SUIT SEPARATES

Leave it to the English shopkeeper to discover a new truth. Years ago, Marks & Spencer, the Macy's of London, made a remarkable discovery—not all men were the same proportion. Some are big on top and narrow in the hips, or, as was more often the case, vice versa. With this eureka moment, the haberdashers launched the concept of suit separates: Pants that fit the waist and a jacket that fit the top, whether the sizes correlated or not. And the concept works even better for women, allowing more flexibility for both size and style. Here is a list of the separates a common business wardrobe will contain.

WHAT TO LOOK FOR

Color: Neutral colors are versatile and professional. Black is sophisticated, appropriate all year, and dresses up or down. Gray, navy, and beige convey competence and easily mix with other clothes. But beware of brown: It is seasonal, can come off as muddy (not meticulous), and is often incompatible with other colors.

Fabric: The more seasonless the fabric, the longer it will serve you. 1. Choose lightweight wool or wool blends that can be worn throughout the year. 2. A bit of Lycra, polyester, or other microfiber helps a garment retain its shape and increases the longevity of your investment. 3. Avoid knits, jerseys, and nubby tweeds for your first and main suit. They're too casual and more difficult to wear with other wardrobe pieces. 4. Before buying, check for wrinkling: Clutch a handful of fabric and release it. If the material winds up in a crumple, it will certainly look that way after your commute to work. 5. Avoid clingy fabrics (some jerseys and knits) and anything with static—chances are no amount of spray will kill it. 6. Pants and skirts in thin fabrics must be lined. If a rearview mirror check displays visible panty lines (or panties), move on to the next suit—or buy a thong!

Fit: Tailoring is mandatory—it's the detail work that will transform your suit from an amorphous mass into an emblem of power. But prior to visiting the tailor, certain key details must be checked: 1. Button the jacket. Does it pull? Do your arms move freely in it? Do the bust, shoulder, and rear seams hang well without bunching? 2. Make sure shoulders are not too round, pointy, or boxy. They shouldn't make the statement, you should. 3. Button the pants and find a three-way mirror. Do you have a panty line? Is the rear too tight? Does the crotch cling or hang too low? A tailor is a great ally, but a baggy or saggy crotch cannot be fixed. An ill-fitting waistline can be taken in, and occasionally let out, if necessary. Sit. Do you feel comfortable or do the pants pull or does your skirt ride too high? And when you shop for pants or visit the tailor bring the shoes you plan to wear with them to get a proper break at the hem.

Quality/Finish: 1. Scan fabric for unnatural ripples or gatherings, which are often the result of inexpensive material and poor workmanship. 2. Make sure shoulder pads are equally positioned and the same size and that the shoulder line is smooth from end to end, front and back. 3. Buttons should be firmly attached and evenly spaced, with no loose threads. 4. Check seams for taut stitching that is neither loose nor pulled. 5. Lining should be made from a satiny material that allows for body movement.

SHOP SMART: SHIRTS

- Fabric is not so sheer that underwear or body parts are noticeable.
- Collar should not be overly large nor especially small. An average collar should be approximately 2$1/2$" from the collar point.
- Buttons should be bone, mother-of-pearl, or animal horn.

- Avoid frilly collars and sleeves, which tend to flop out from under a jacket.
- Length must be ample enough to stay tucked in, but not so extreme that you're swimming in fabric.
- When cuffs are buttoned, you should be able to move arms comfortably.

Fit: Should not be too baggy, but definitely not tight. Bra line, breast, or nipple definition should not be apparent. Cotton is the most practical fabric and comes in a wide variety of grades and texture:
- Egyptian: smooth, silky, most expensive.
- Pima: strong, silky.
- Sea Island: strong and lustrous.
- Oxford cloth: men's shirting fabric made in a basket weave; considered sporty.

Silk is dressier than cotton.

SHOP SMART: SHOES

Comfort: Work shoes are not show-piece stilettos. Action is required. Find a heel height and toe shape that are easy to walk in. Never buy shoes that feel tight. It's better to shop for shoes at the end of the day when your feet have slightly expanded. Neither mules nor open-toe shoes are suitable in the workplace.

Quality: Don't skimp on quality, but you don't have to break the bank. Choose a classic design in a dark leather. Black is most versatile.
- Avoid shoes with obvious seams; they cheapen the look of the entire shoe.
- Inspect the way the shoe is finished. Edges should be smooth, not frayed. Leather should be supple, not stiff.
- Heels must be the same color as the shoe—not metallic, contrasting, or paler, stacked heels.

Shape:
- A low vamp (or top of the shoe) lengthens the look of the leg. A high vamp shortens the leg. It should not be cut so low as to expose toe cleavage.
- A low-cut pump with a low or medium, narrow heel is most flattering.
- Heel shape often dates a shoe. Look for a trim, sculpted heel, nothing chunky or trendy.
- Black pumps with a chiseled heel are appropriate in a formal work environment or at a dressy business dinner.

Maintenance:
- Wooden shoe trees help maintain the shape of the shoe.
- Polish frequently.
- Have shoes reheeled and resoled before they get run-down.
- For rain-soaked shoes, stuff with newspaper during drying to help maintain shape.
- Shoes exposed to salt may be wiped clean up to eight hours before the leather begins to oxidize. After that time, try treating damaged area with diluted white vinegar.

SHOP SMART: HOSIERY

- Sheer textures are more formal than opaque yet tear easily, so stick with an inexpensive brand. Keep an extra pair in your desk drawer just in case.
- When buying nude hosiery, test the color against your inner forearm, which tends to be closest in color to your leg.
- Hose can be lighter than shoes, but never darker. Shoes can be darker than dress or skirt, but not lighter.
- When in doubt, match skirt, hose,

and shoes—the less contrast, the more lengthening the look.
- With sheer black, make sure fit is precise so color is evenly distributed on the leg.
- Dark opaque hose are best in winter, slimming to the leg, and most often paired with casual looks.
- The sportier the shoe, the more opaque the hose. The dressier the shoe, the sheerer the hose.
- A variety of control panels are available—from athletic-looking girdles to all-over elastic leggings.
- Reinforced toes and heels promote durability and longevity (but don't let them near open-toe sandals).

Socks:
- Color should be consistent with your wardrobe palette, echoing the color of your pants or shoes.
- Socks should rise high enough that, when seated, no leg gapes beneath pant cuff.
- When buying basics, buy several pairs of the same in case you lose a single sock.
- Avoid drying socks (or panty hose) in the dryer. Heat destroys the elastic.

SHOP SMART: BAG
Black is authoritative and versatile.
Texture: Leather conveys quality. Smooth is more polished but may show wear more easily than a rugged pebbled finish.
Style: Keep it classic. Subtle if any hardware, and no prints, or other extraneous details.
Utility:
- Check for dividers and zipped pockets that aid in organization. Pawing through a cluttered, oversized bag conjures scatterbrain stereotypes.

- For maximum strength, seams should be piped or bound.
- Straps should be double sided with no stray threads.
- Buy the best quality you can afford. A good bag can be polished and repaired for years. A cheap one will wear out quickly.
- Price does not equal quality. Often you are paying for a designer's name. Check that the workmanship is precise and well finished, the stitching is solid, the zippers function smoothly, and snaps remain closed.
- The size of your bag should be compatible with the size of your frame.
- Matching shoes to handbag is no longer required, though they should be compatible.

SHOP SMART: JEWELRY
Work jewelry should be simple and minimal. You may want to establish a personal style such as wearing the same string of pearls every day. Whatever look you decide upon it should be of good quality, not trendy, and understated. Wear a single strand, and make sure the clasp is discreet.
Pearls:
- Pearls are inherently organic; they must be worn in order to keep their luster and are damaged by perfume.
- Real pearls should be strung with knots between them in case the strand breaks.
- The best lengths to bring focus to your face rather than your bust:
    Choker: 14–16 inches. This is the most classic and versatile look, great with all necklines and with outfits casual to formal.
    Princess: 17–19 inches. This length is best suited for crew,

high, and plunging necklines (an office no-no).
- Excellent faux pearls are better than cultured pearls of inferior quality. Remember, the pearl shape should be round.
- Faux pearls are made with beads of shell nacre or opalescent glass covered by dissolved fish scale extract or other luster-inducing substances. Unlike the fakes of yore, they peel like real pearls, and don't break easily.
- Quality in cultured pearls is determined by a pearl's "orient," or the soft iridescent light from within (created by layers of shell nacre), as well as size, thickness of nacre layers, cleanliness, and color.
- To determine authenticity, gently rub the pearls against your teeth. If they are real, they will feel slightly gritty, rather than smooth like faux pearls.

Gold: The purer the gold, the more expensive it will be. Pure gold (24 karat) is too soft to be used for jewelry. Fourteen-karat gold is standard.
Silver: Keep it polished, which is easy with silver jewelry cleaner that only requires dipping pieces in for seconds, then wiping dry.

SHOP SMART: GLASSES
Professional-looking frames should be black, tortoiseshell, brown, wire rims, or rimless.
If you wear glasses regularly consider:
- A simple metal or tortoiseshell chain. No flashy beads or colors.
- An eyeglass case that is structured and brightly colored, which makes it easier to find in your bag.

1. Get Job

Countdown for the Job Interview

**SWEET SMELL
OF SUCCESS**
Avoid all noticeable scents
and smells, from overpow-
ering fragrances to body
odor and bad breath.
Perfume should be a subtle
accent to your personality,
not a personality unto itself.

DRESSING TO GET THE JOB

The suit may have taken some slack during the dot-com dressed-down era, but now job competition is high, business is fierce, and looking shipshape and in fighting form matters.

THE POWER OF A LIST

Architect Mies Van der Rohe said, "God is in the details." If you can summon such divine power simply by conquering the little things, you better make a list. List everything. In the days leading up to your interview, list each item you will need to wear (suit, undergarments, shoes, hosiery, accessories, watch…). List related tasks you need to accomplish (polish shoes, get manicure). List what you need to bring (notepad to jot key points and questions, extra résumés). List the questions you might be asked and your best answers. List the questions you want to ask (job description specifics, 401[k] timetable). Review your lists as often as you can stand until the big day arrives.

PREINTERVIEW: DRESS REHEARSAL

A week before your interview, put everything on. Make sure tailoring is satisfactory. Make sure your stockings fit comfortably and match your shoes and skirt. Make sure you can sit down in your skirt and that it doesn't ride up. Make sure résumés fit in your portfolio.

Preparation breeds confidence. If you have done your homework you will feel qualified for the job. And it will show. The interviewer will see you as qualified, too, and…

CONGRATULATIONS: THE SECOND INTERVIEW

You're asked back for a second interview. Minor complication: You want to make another impression, but you have only one interview suit. Find out who this meeting is with. If the first meeting was with the key player, the second one is usually with other subplayers whose jobs will cross paths with yours. If this is the case, and it's not a formal business setting, it is a formal business meeting. Create a look by mixing up the suit: You might lose the jacket and wear the skirt with a sweater set. Or wear the jacket with a pair of neutral tailored pants.

ENOUGH ALREADY: THE THIRD CALLBACK

The third interview is often the last. It means you're meeting with the boss, whose ultimate decision your hiring falls to. If it is, revert back to your suit, but wear it differently—try a new shirt or blouse underneath, in a bright color, or add a scarf around the neck. A slight tweak of one or two details will keep you looking fresh.

SPECIAL CIRCUMSTANCES: BREAKFAST, LUNCH, DINNER, OTHERS

If lunch with the future boss sounds like a picnic, it's not. It's still an interview, and even more of a test because your social skills, table manners, and even talent for banter can all come into scrutinized play. Not only that, the off-site interview tends to activate a whole new set of dress code paranoia. Remember: It's still an interview, and you should wear whatever you would have worn had the meeting been in an office. Unless the CEO has an affection for Arby's, your interview attire will fit right in at whatever establishment you are asked to meet.

BE PREPARED
Employers say that candidates who manage to land interviews are increasingly unprepared—sometimes woefully so—for the interviewing process. "Many can't provide details to probing questions," said Paige Soltano, senior partner for Bozell New York, an advertising agency. "If they tell you they completed a successful project at their old job, and you ask them why it was successful, they aren't able to give any details."
New York Times
8/8/01

Interview Wardrobe

The clothes you choose to wear to your interview will create the first—and most important—impression upon those who matter, up until your first day on the job. At that point, you can start to relax into the club's attire. But at this point, dressing to impress is mandatory, and the clothes you choose are critical. This section discusses the interview wardrobe's key pieces, and the messages they send.

"At one time, the most qualified person got the job. Today, in a situation where three people with equal qualifications are interviewed for a job, the one with the best communication skills gets it."

ROGER AILES
You Are the Message

WHAT DO YOUR CLOTHES SAY TO THE INTERVIEWER?

BLOUSE
Uptight
or
Elegant?

PEARLS
Pretentious
or
Pulled together?

SUIT JACKET
A sensible snooze
or
Sophisticated?

HEM
Boring
or
Professional?

Suit Jacket

Long ago pilfered from menswear (and originally adapted from medieval armor), the jacket acts as a strong, no-nonsense centerpiece to any business look. It gives the body shape, suggests stature, and imparts the wearer with confidence. Because its overall intent is to convey power, a jacket's workmanship, quality, and tailoring are critical.

FABRIC
Should drape smoothly, not appear stiff, shiny, or flimsy.

COLOR
Neutral—black, gray, navy, or beige.

SHAPE
Slightly nipped in at waist.

POCKETS
Optional pockets lie flat and are lined. Do not remove string to open.

LENGTH
Hem extends to the bottom of the hips.

SLEEVES
Sleeves land at the base of the thumb.

COLLAR
Collar lies smooth and
flat against the neck.

SHOULDERS
Shoulders are structured
but not overpadded.

LAPELS
Medium to small lapels
($3^1/4$" from seam to point
is ideal) lie flat without
buckling.

FIT
Armholes should fit well—
not too baggy, not too tight;
this part of the jacket can't
be tailored.

STYLE
Single-breasted.

BUTTONS
Buttons are the same color
or darker than the suit and
never too large, flashy, or
covered in fabric.

Suit Skirt

WHAT IT SAYS

Formal, urban, conservative.

FABRIC

Drapes smoothly.

NO BELT LOOPS

Means maximum versatility.

SHAPE

Simple—A-line or straight, not too tight
and never frilly.

DETAILS

For maximum versatility, the waist should
not require a belt.

FIT

Skirt should not be too tight or too short—do a
sitting test in it before purchasing. Check the
rearview mirror. What looks fabulous from the
front can cling or slouch from other angles.

QUALITY

Make sure seams are even and not pulled.
Check that the lining is firmly intact.

LENGTH

To the knee. It's the length that says,
"I'm professional" and looks best on
most legs. Shorter could be considered
too fashiony; longer, more traditional.

Suit Pants

WHAT IT SAYS
Confident, contemporary, practical.

FIT
Pants should drape smoothly over the body, with no tight areas that pull, no baggy areas that droop. Check that the pocket lining is smooth and not bulky.

QUALITY
Check that fabric hangs evenly and seams are not mismatched or pulled.

THE BOTTOM LINE
The seat of the pants should be neither overly baggy nor clingy. To ensure proper fit, check your rearview mirror and sit down while wearing the pants.

ZIP CODE
Side, front, or rear closure are acceptable.

BANISH BELT LOOPS
For your first suit, a clean waistline is the most flexible. Belt loops always require a belt and that your top is tucked in.

FLAT FRONT VS. PLEATS
Both are professional; the flat front is more slimming and sophisticated.

LENGTH
The pant leg should break at the instep. When having your pants hemmed, bring the shoe you will most often wear with them.

CUFFED LEG VS. CLEAN
Both are acceptable; a clean leg is more versatile.

Tops are key wardrobe enhancers: Change your top and essentially you've changed your look. Choose shirts and blouses that are compatible with your suits. Make sure each top fits comfortably under your suit jacket—and looks suitably professional should you take your jacket off.

BLOUSE
A soft, somewhat loose feminine top. Conservative, confident, ladylike.
FIRST PURCHASE: Solid white, cream, black, or a color to match your suit.

SHIRT
Button-front, cuffed-and-collared top inspired by menswear.
Efficient, classic; respects authority. Choose a classic, men's
style dress collar; a button-down can be limiting.
FIRST PURCHASE: Solid, white cotton.

Tops

FITTED T-SHIRT

Trim, collarless, cotton or jersey top. Easygoing but organized. Ready to roll up your sleeves (since they already are…). Choose substantial, opaque cotton or cotton blend with stretch—anything flimsy will lose its shape. Make sure neck is not saggy or baggy. Keep it plain (this is not your U2 concert T-shirt). Try a shot of color.

FIRST PURCHASE: Solid white, black, or to match the color of your suit.

1 JACKET + 4 TOPS

CORPORATE

For a corporate interview, your suit and the gear that goes with it must leave no doubt that you are polished, professional, and supremely qualified for the job. For the first interview, wear an impeccably tailored skirt suit with a white blouse, heels, hose, and perhaps pearls.

CORPORATE

For the second corporate interview, trade shirts (gray on gray is suitably subdued), and consider switching to pants, if appropriate.

= 3 DRESS CODES

BUSINESS APPROPRIATE

A slightly more relaxed workplace does not mean more relaxed interview clothes. Any first meeting requires dressing for success. Wear a suit; whether it's with pants or a skirt is your choice. A crisp white shirt and pearls give a sleek suit a no-nonsense authoritative edge.

CASUAL

A relatively slack dress code does not apply to the interview. Look pulled together and professional, whether or not you will dress remotely like that on the job. A gray suit jacket kicks back without slacking off when worn with a quality white T-shirt and pearls.

Shoes

Heels should be three inches or less; higher screams siren, not CEO.

Classic toe. Not too pointy, overly round or square.

HIGH-HEELED CLASSIC PUMP
Traditional, professional, formal. Works day and night. Wear with skirts and pants. Pant leg must be long enough to break over the instep.
FIRST PURCHASE: Black leather. It's strong, seasonless, and works with everything, dressy or relaxed.

LOAFER

Down-to-earth, practical. Wear only with trousers. Keep in excellent condition (no prep-school scuffs or pennies). Pick a style with minimal or no detail—a small metal bar is acceptable. For hosiery, choose trouser socks that match the shoe or pant color.

Stitching should match color of shoe.

A loafer's high vamp makes it a strong finish to a pantsuit.

Never underestimate the power of shoes. A good pair can make a ho-hum dress look like a million bucks. The wrong ones can send a great suit straight into the gutter. Shoes also tend to make at-a-glance statements about your workplace identity, and your message better be clear—I'm capable, confident, and, ycs, great with details.

Minimal or no detail.

MIDHEIGHT, BLOCK-HEELED PUMP

Polished, competent, no-nonsense. Pair with skirts, trousers, or dresses—this shoe is highly versatile. With a skirt, wear with opaque or semiopaque hosiery. With pants, wear with opaque trouser socks. This heel is too heavy to pair with delicate sheers. Match hosiery to shoe or pant color.

Socks

TROUSER SOCK
Medium-weight socks worn with loafers and slacks. It is more sporty than the dress sock, and lighter in weight than a sport sock. The dressier the pant, the more silky the texture required.

COLOR
Avoid patterns. Match sock shade to shoe or pant color if neutral.

DRESS SOCK
Lightweight silky hosiery worn when dressier trousers are paired with a feminine shoe.

LOAFER + TROUSER = TROUSER SOCK

MIDHEEL + TROUSER = DRESS SOCK

and Hose

One of the most frequently asked questions we get at www.chicsimple.com is about hosiery. Is it always necessary to wear? What color or texture looks best with a particular outfit or shoe? In the interview, the answer is simple: Hosiery is always required. The only acceptable colors are nude and black (solid, sheer, or semisheer).

OPAQUE BLACK

Urban, practical, creative, relaxed. Wear during fall and winter with skirts or dresses of substantial weight (not wispy silk). Pair with dark shoes that are not too delicate.

SHEER BLACK

Polished, sophisticated, dressy. Wear for day and at evening events with clothes that are somewhat dressy or formal. Choose shoes that are relatively delicate, like a heeled classic pump.

NUDE

Conservative. In formal work environments, wear with skirts and dresses of any weight and color.

Portfolio

A portfolio is a sleek and efficient alternative to the handbag. It can help keep résumés presentable, hold a notepad, and conceal any preinterview cheat sheets you want to study en route to your meeting.

Organized, presentable, prepared. A neat, tidy design (no neon colors, action heroes, or unicorns) in leather or a techno-texture like matte plastic.

A sturdy material will ensure résumés will not become creased.

Leather is a sign of quality and sophistication.

Extra pocket for supreme organization.

Purse

A bag carries strong connotations about its wearer. Does yours send a businesslike vibe to your potential employer?

FIRST PURCHASE

Black leather. It's authoritative and versatile.

Make sure straps on a shoulder bag are not too long. Bag should not hang below your waist.

Keep hardware to a minimum.

Bag must be neatly zipped. It conveys organization and control.

INTERVIEW CHECKLIST

The must-carry equipment that will prepare you for anything when heading out for an interview.

- ❏ 2 pens (in case one runs out)
- ❏ Notepad (to jot down key points or questions)
- ❏ Wallet
- ❏ Name, address, and phone number of interview location
- ❏ Extra résumés (always seem to be required; name and address should be at the top)
- ❏ Folder for résumés (to avoid crumpling)
- ❏ List of references
- ❏ Calendar (to schedule next appointment or start date)
- ❏ Cell phone (switch off before interview) and quarters in case cell phone isn't operating
- ❏ Breath mints
- ❏ Tissues
- ❏ Mirror (to check teeth for lipstick, seek out stray hairs, etc.)
- ❏ Lipstick
- ❏ Comb
- ❏ Extra hosiery (for a quick switch in case of a run)
- ❏ Mini-shoe-buffer (scuffs say sloppy)
- ❏ Handiwipes (for last-minute stains)
- ❏ Nail file (to deliver a jab-free handshake)

Watch

In the workplace, the way you manage time denotes efficiency, or a lack thereof. A business watch should be classic and discreet, and a good-looking one doesn't have to break the bank.

STAINLESS STEEL GOLD WATCH

=

DECORATIVE, OUTGOING, ASSERTIVE.

Easy to read, but not digital, which is too sporty.

Round or rectangular face are equally appropriate.

A versatile, stainless steel and gold combination matches both gold and silver jewelry.

Asset: Date indicator.

Integral bracelet.

Light-colored background face.

Link, not expansion, band.

ROUND-FACED LEATHER WATCH

=

CONSERVATIVE, PRACTICAL, NO-NONSENSE, STRAIGHTFORWARD.

Check for proper fit. Watch should firmly grasp the wrist and not slide around like a bracelet.

Substantial bezel.

Single dial.

Asset: Illuminating face.

Substantial lug.

Padded leather band.

Don't supersize.

TREND ALERT

At work, a watch is a watch, not jewelry. Things to avoid in the office: Colored faces, bright-colored bands, contrasting stitching, and an oversized face.

Glasses and

Your glasses shouldn't make a bigger statement than you do. Choose eyewear that is polished and professional. And if you don't wear glasses, consider them: Some devoted careerists with perfect vision wear them with nonprescription lenses as a brainy accessory. Just keep in mind: The size of the frames should match your features, not overwhelm your face. Stick to simple shapes and clear lenses.

Jewelry

Jewelry is optional. Should you choose to wear it, keep it simple. It should neither overpower your look nor provide a soundtrack (in other words, no noisy bangle bracelets). The office is not the place to flaunt the family jewels. Less is more.

WIRE RIMS =
DISCREET, THOUGHTFUL, UNDERSTATED

TORTOISESHELL FRAMES =
REFINED, STUDIOUS, CLASSIC

HORN RIMS =
ATTITUDE, EDGY, HIP

SMART OPTIONS:
- Small diamond, pearl, gold, or silver stud earrings or small hoops.
- A single strand of pearls, or a delicate gold or silver necklace.
- A bracelet may be overkill with your watch, but if you insist keep it singular and subtle, not an orchestra of them.

BACK TRACKING
When an earring back wanders off, a slice of a pencil eraser acts as an effective stand-in.

CLOSET interview wardrobe

At this early stage of your career, the "work" zone of your closet will be, understandably, sparse. It's a perfect time to learn the key to closet planning: Organization. After all, you can't wear what you can't see. Here, the clothes, accessories, and organizational gear your career closet should contain:

INTERVIEW WARDROBE

- 1 suit
- 5 tops
- 2 pairs of shoes
- 1 handbag
- 1 leather portfolio
- 1 watch
- hosiery
- undergarments

CLOSET TOOLS

- Full-length mirror
- Good lighting (closet and the mirror)
- Sturdy hangers (maintain condition of your clothes)
- Shoe trees (ditto for shoes)
- Lint remover
- Iron
- Steamer
- Spot remover

CLOTHES CHECK

- Avoid dry-cleaning your garments frequently: It's hard on fabrics (worn often—biweekly; worn once a week—monthly; worn occasionally—seasonally).
- Use spot remover as an alternative.
- To air out clothes after wearing, hang garments for 24 hours before putting back in the closet. This may also help to shake out wrinkles.
- When you dry-clean garments, which is smart before you stow things away for out-of-season storage, dry-clean suit pieces together. Otherwise the color or finish may no longer match.
- Always remove cleaned items from plastic cleaner bags. They tend to yellow whites, hold in moisture, and are somewhat toxic.

OFF THE MOMMY TRACK

Dear Kim and jeff,
I have forgotten how to dress. For eight years I have been a stay-at-home
mom. Before, I worked in corporate affairs at a large insurance company
near Chicago. I took time out to have my two girls and just got a job in
the communications department of an airline company. I'm excited
about the job but I'm frantically bouncing between a suit I bought for
job hunting and my one dress-up outfit from my mommy days. Help! I
just can't seem to get started. I just can't afford to make any mistakes.
—Closet Challenged

Dear Closet Challenged,
Your next best investment should be another suit, but make sure it's
versatile, and that it can be worn with the same shoes and bag that you
wear with your other suit. After that, buy a few different tops to wear
with your different suit bottoms. Consider a sweater set as it is a feminine yet professional alternative to a suit jacket.

—Kim and jeff

Succeed in Job 2

Work Wardrobe

This is simple: There are three workers sitting around a table. A senior executive approaches with a project, a problem that needs solving. Instantly, each of the three people has a shot at what might be an important turning point in her career. A decision will be made, and only one will be chosen. How can you make an impression so that you are the one? In this section, you will learn how to build a wardrobe to ensure that when the moment arrives, you will be ready.

2. Succeed in Job

Dress Like You Mean Business

> "I want to know why, if men rule the world, they don't stop wearing neckties."
>
> **LINDA ELLERBEE**
> Writer, producer, President of Lucky Duck Productions

DRESSING FOR THE JOB

To Carolyn Lantz, image is everything. As executive director of brand imaging at the Ford Motor Company—involved with creative tasks from the design of the cars to the ad campaigns that go with them—she and her department are the imaginative rebels of the century-old, blue-chip company. And they better dress like it, or else. "One of my designers has blue hair, another dresses surf city. They're obsessed with the latest trends, and they should be," she says. "Twice a year we have the CEO and group vice presidents here, and I forbid anyone from wearing a suit. They put us in California, not Detroit, because they wanted us to think differently, outside the box that is the automotive industry, and to be creative. If we looked like Detroit they're going to wonder why we're on such a mainstream wavelength."

A new head designer of Lantz's was asked to speak to students at MIT; she went out and bought a new suit for the occasion. "This was a brilliant designer, and a good speaker, and the students just sat there rolling their eyes. I think they were thinking, 'Oh, another suit from Detroit,' " she says. "Afterwards, when we were alone, I said, 'Your claim to fame is you're creative and you're pretty brilliant at what you do. I think you've got the right to be more expressive.' In the end, despite the colorful message of the talk, the stiffness of the suit was the bigger signal to the audience."

In an interview, goal number one is to wear clothes that convey professionalism. Once you have the job, however, a host of nuances and variables enter into the picture that must be taken into account if you want to be successful in your position.

YOUR WORK WARDROBE—ENSURING IMAGE CONTROL

Whether it's suspenders at certain Wall Street firms, a camel blazer in real estate, or dark denim in Hollywood, every job has its fashion slang. What subtleties does your position demand? Below is a checklist of prerequisites to be interpreted for your particular position/office/industry. Each day, the clothes you wear should be:

1. Appropriate. An office/industry is a club. Look like you belong.

2. Professional. Clothes that are suitably businesslike, whether that means corporate, business appropriate, or business casual, will give you the confidence that comes with dressing the part.

3. Comfortable. Dress for your position, personality, and body.

4. Strategic. A well-thought-out wardrobe can help you fulfill your goals. Are you an assistant looking for a promotion? Start to dress more in the mode of your superiors. In a traditional profession where a formal dress code has everyone looking like clones? Mix splashes of color with the dress code, using a pale blue sweater or a beautiful scarf to set yourself apart with individual flair. Take into account your goals, your field, what rung of the ladder you're on, and even where on the map you are, and determine whether you're dressing as smart as you could.

BEING APPROPRIATE—ONE LESS THING TO WORRY ABOUT

If you take the initial time and effort to make your wardrobe as ship-shape as your memos to the CEO, both you and your memos will be taken more seriously. You can get dressed in the morning, enter the staff meeting with the group VP, and enjoy a lunch meeting with clients, knowing you look professional and prepared.

Fail to take this initial action and, along with the stress you feel about your meetings, memos, quotas, power points, and marketing strategies, add a nonstop, underlying doubt as to whether your clothes are appropriate and up to snuff. Anyone who can endure such exhausting worry is worthy of CEO status. If only she looked the part.

RUN OF THE OFFICE
It's a pain, but corporate, and even some business appropriate, dress codes still insist on hose when in the office.

$2.$ Succeed in Job

Do You Dress for Job or Career?

LEARNING FROM MEN
Not everything they do is worth stealing, but we'll take the blazer. The notion of a "bulletproof" piece of clothing that instantly pulls you together—no matter how late you were out the night before or how temperamental the nanny—is genius. Find one perfect, dark-colored blazer and wear it to death. Men do.

EVERY DAY IS AN OPPORTUNITY. ARE YOU DRESSED FOR IT?
Anthea Disney is the CEO of News America Publishing Group, and, for the most part, she wears the same thing she wore on the first day of her first job as a London newspaper reporter. "It's always been some semblance of a suit—a pantsuit and a crisp shirt or a sweater, or black pants, a turtleneck, and a leather jacket. I think the uniform I came up with was respectable but anonymous," she says. "The only time I remember anyone commenting on my clothes was when a superior said: 'You dress like you know who you are.'"

Disney's look was respectable enough that, no matter who she ran into, and no matter how high her aspirations soared, her clothes helped support her ambitions. "I was an editor of a magazine [*US*, *TV Guide*], an executive producer [Fox-TV's *A Current Affair*], and I've been a CEO [HarperCollins Publishers]. And all along I've pretty much worn the same thing. It's who I am and how I feel comfortable."

In each instance, her polished look was a signal to higher-ups that she had the reliability and strength to tackle the task at hand.

What would your clothes say to those in a position to give you a promotion or fulfill your next dream? Careers are made through day-to-day tasks and impressions, not on the day of the job review. Every day is an interview for the next step in your life. Your clothes will either hold you back or help you soar.

Didn't Get the Memo

THE TIMES ARE CHANGING, ARE YOU?

First George W. Bush banned casual dress at the White House, even on weekends. Then the nation's law firms began objecting to casual Fridays. Even slacker emeritus Bill Gates has been spotted wearing suits and ties. When the economy is soaring, every day is Friday, and the dress code chills out accordingly. But when times turn tough, the pace quickens, and everyone shows up early, sits up straight, dresses as if their lives depended on it. After seasons in a slump, suit sales are soaring again, and offices around the nation are once again running like clockwork and looking shipshape. Did you get the memo?

LOOK AROUND—WHO DID GET THE MEMO?

A scan around the office can provide a good indication of the demeanor, both professional and sartorial, and where you stand. Who's wearing what? Has your boss, who had begun experimenting with denim, quietly decided that that's not such a good idea? Is your colleague in the next cubicle suddenly sporting a suit—every day? One telling lesson is that most CEOs (aka supremely experienced business people) never stopped wearing suits, having learned that it's one detail they can't afford to overlook, no matter what the economy.

Still schlumping around in your Friday casual garb? This could be the time to consider dressing a little smarter.

2. Succeed in Job

Strategic Dressing
—Learning to Read the Landscape

MENTOR RULES

A latest job accessory for the female careerist isn't a chic leather portfolio or the newest laptop. It's a same-gender mentor. And among the many valuable lessons this guide can impart to her protégée are the rules of the dress code road. Still, times change and subtleties develop quickly. Take what you think works and ignore the rest.

CLOTHES QUARTERS—WHO LOOKS PROFESSIONAL AND WHAT ARE THEY WEARING

What does dressing smart mean in your office? Dress codes tend to trickle down, so start your examination at the top. What is the CEO wearing? A skirt suit, Hermès scarf, and heels? Translation: This office aspires to formal corporate attire. Does the creative team wear dark denim, blazers, and loafers but the financiers wear pinstripe suits and heels? Determine where you fit into your office's clothes spectrum and navigate your personal dress code accordingly.

What does your boss wear? If your boss is respected and in good standing at the company—and is someone whose character and career you would like to emulate—then it's a good idea to take the way she dresses as a role model. Work toward approximating the look as best as you can on your budget. If she tends to wear suits, you might focus expanding that area of your own closet. If it's a more casual office where personal style comes into play, use the way she dresses to help determine the boundaries: She wears leather but not denim, and always wears heels.

THE NEW BUSINESS LOOK: BUSINESS APPROPRIATE

If your office isn't a sea of suits or a gaggle of khakis, chances are it's "business appropriate." A dress code that evolved to bridge the gap between "casual" and "corporate," a business appropriate look has the

• 66 •

"I don't care what you look like before 9 and after 5. Put purple in your hair, expose your midriff, pierce everything. But I run a billion-dollar company, and I want that company to look like a billion bucks."

JANE FRIEDMAN
CEO, HarperCollins Publishing

professional polish of a suit, but takes the edge off. In other words, a suit is not always required. Common examples of this middle-of-the-road dress code—which is quickly becoming the most common one in the country—are a blazer with contrasting pants and a blouse; a skirt and a sweater set; a turtleneck and trousers, with a nice belt (if the pants have loops).

DRESSING WITH YOUR CALENDAR

Different work situations require different messages. Scan your calendar to determine which clothes will send the right message that day:
10 A.M. Staff meeting. (Desired effect: Approachable yet authoritative.)
1 P.M. Lunch with boss. (Desired effect: Whiz kid?)
3 P.M. Coffee with clients. (Desired effect: Serious business.)

Leading the Meeting: A suit says authority, the single most important quality when leading a meeting. While choosing the look of a laid-back-and-approachable leader is always an option—say, a turtleneck and pants instead of a suit—only those extremely confident should venture here. This tactic risks having others in the meeting being more dressed up—and more authoritative—than you are.

Making the Presentation: When giving a presentation, the key is to draw attention to yourself, as long as it's positive and the proper amount. As with any public appearance, a suit gives the body a distinct shape and a strong physical outline. An interesting color is attractive and lively and energetic: Pale blue or red. Avoid anything that's eye-catching to the point of distraction: Dangling earrings, striped or polka-dot scarves, blinding colors.

Client Lunch: At a client lunch, you want to come across as professional, reliable, and at the same time approachable. Closet translation: A suit worn with something to ease its stiffness, whether that's the suit's inviting color (white, cream, or pale blue), or a T-shirt you wear under it, or a piece of personal jewelry, such as a pendant or pin.

Job Review: When faced with a job review, you want to look the way you would on your best day at the office. If you ever wear a suit on the job, then a suit is in order. If you don't, do not wear one just for this occasion. It will look contrived. The goal is to look professional and relaxed and not as though you're trying too hard.

A Chic Simple Review
—Revisit Your Goals

"No woman can be well dressed unless she is comfortable in what she is wearing."

BILL BLASS

Goals evolve, industries change. Now that you've been in your job for a while, is your career—and your closet—supporting your goals?

ASSESS: ARE YOU WHERE YOU WANT TO BE?
Look at your career: Do you enjoy your work? Is it consistent with your goals? Do you like where you see yourself landing in five years? Look in your closet: Does getting dressed every day make you comfortable? Are your clothes consistent with the way you see yourself? With the person you'd like to be in five years?

DEJUNK: WHAT IS HOLDING YOU BACK?
If you're not happy, determine why. Are you clinging to an old notion of your industry? Is your style of dress dated and restrictive? Have you become stuck in a niche that isn't you? Does your image reinforce your junior placement? Are your wardrobe choices holding you back?

RENEW: FOCUS ON THE GOALS YOU'VE MADE
Take steps to adjust your career path to suit your revised goals. Start adapting your closet to support your new game plan: If it's more structure you seek, up the suit quotient. If it's more self-expression, try a few pieces in dramatic colors, or trendy shoes. These small steps will keep you headed in a direction that satisfies your changing career goals.

The ROI Wardrobe
—Return On Investment

CLASSIC INVESTMENT
The more classic the jewelry, the more versatile. That means simple lines and timeless design, and a subtlety that won't cause people to say, "Oh, she's wearing the… again." And remember: Classic doesn't have to mean boring.

STRETCHING A WARDROBE

"I used to buy two Armani suits a year, and that would take up my whole budget," says book publisher and TV talk show host Judith Regan. "So I'd have to be extremely creative with them—I'd change blouses, have the suits dry-cleaned 400 times, have the shoulder pads taken out or put back in. But I always felt I looked right."

At the start of a career, most people won't be decked out in Armani. But they are likely to face an all-too-common dilemma: "Help, I only have one suit (or two). What do I wear tomorrow?"

With a little creativity, the two pieces of a suit can be stretched to create a plethora of office ensembles (MIT engineers reading this book can do the logarithms, though many are off the hook when it comes to business dressing—they're called lab coats). Worn with well-chosen extras, a versatile suit can morph into 12 different looks or more: Pair the jacket with three different pairs of pants (black, gray, a color, or even white jeans, if they're allowed) and three different skirts; wear the pants with five different tops—a crisp white shirt, a sweater set, a turtleneck, a silk blouse, and maybe a different jacket; then wear the suit as a whole. Other transformers: A colorful scarf (or two), a bright colored top, something denim (if kosher in your office), different accessories—wear a suit with pearls one day (classic), a T-shirt the next (cool), a T-shirt with pearls (cool classic).

2. Succeed in Job

BUTTON UP
Don't let an ugly brass button—or one that's the wrong shade, size, or shininess—ruin a jacket or suit. This is where a tailor can change your life, or at least your day. With the addition of some well-chosen buttons, a suit can take on a whole new life.

INVESTING IN YOUR FUTURE
Dressing smart requires: A moderate outlay of cash and a strategy. Establishing your career—and closet—strategies now will have an impact on your professional life every hour of every day you are on the job. The initial investment of well-spent time and money will be returned a thousandfold. Besides, you can look like a million bucks without spending it.

UNDERSTANDING NECESSARY EXPENDITURES
Things to keep in mind when formulating your work wardrobe:
1. You might already own a lot of what you need.
2. Choose one (possibly two) key items to invest in, usually your suit, and spend less on everything else. As your salary increases, so will the number of investment items in your closet.
3. Saviors for the budget minded: Seasonal sales, sample sales, designer outlets. (Be careful of the latter; they can be filled with irregulars, seconds, or clothes never intended for regular retail outlets.)
4. Decide what you choose to invest in: A suit. A watch. A coat.
5. Decide what to skimp on: Shoes–if you're hard on them, you may want to spend less, but buy more frequently. Shirts (a crisp white shirt is that, at any price). Tees with stretch. Anything black (black looks more expensive than its colorful counterparts).

THE POWER OF DETAIL
Accents can make an outfit. When in doubt, wear a black or partial black base, and transform it with accessories and color: A pretty sweater, a colorful scarf, a string of pearls, a feminine blouse, cuff links on a white shirt, a quality handbag, different shoes.

IT'S NOT WHAT YOU SPEND, IT'S WHAT YOU WEAR
Dressing smart means a clear message, a precise fit (courtesy of a good tailor), appropriate details, proper grooming, and the confidence that comes with the fulfillment of all of the above. An ill-fitting, poorly carried expensive suit can come off as a disaster, while an inexpensive one that's perfectly tailored with great shoes and crisp shirt can mean serious business.

Shop Smart: Building a Business Wardrobe
—Your Investment Strategy

WHAT IT TAKES TO BUILD A WARDROBE

- It takes time.
- It takes focus.
- It takes patience.
- It takes work.
- It takes restraint.
- It takes self-knowledge.
- It takes a budget.
- It takes boldness.
- It takes enterprise.
- It takes commitment.

SHOP SMART: BUY LESS, BUY BETTER

This step in the wardrobe building process is important: Clothes take up real estate. And salary. The key is to buy less, buy better, and buy clothes that will work together. Filling your closet with well-chosen, good quality, versatile pieces will enable you to "work" your wardrobe by mixing and remixing. The result: Endless combinations that don't require an endless supply of clothes.

Buy the best you can afford on your budget. You'll go home with fewer items, but they will be of better quality. This is especially important when purchasing items worn every day—coats, shoes, handbags—the better the quality, the bigger your return will be. In general:

- Clothes in seasonless fabrics are the best investment. They can be worn most of the year, and pack well. The best are lightweight wools and wool blends, with a bit of stretch, and lightweight knits.
- Don't buy the color of the moment if it makes your face look drab or your body bulky. Wear it as an accent strategically placed.
- If a color gives you a glow, and makes you smile with approval, incorporate it into your wardrobe mix. Not only will you feel best wearing it, it will become a mark of your personal style.
- One very good quality item can upgrade almost any outfit.
- When you find a brand that suits you, chances are it will continue to be a good shopping resource for you in the future.

shop smart

The goal: To broaden your closet with wardrobe enhancers (well-chosen items that go with other clothes in your closet and expand their possibilities immeasurably). Among the enhancers of choice: A smattering of shirts and blouses (to go under jackets and spruce up skirts), sweater sets and other bright knits, and tailored separates that take the pressure off the single suit that helped you soar through your early years with flying colors (or neutral ones, anyway).

How to Buy a Work Outfit

SHOP SMART: THE JACKET

A jacket is professional in appearance and pulls an outfit together. It is also a good way to add color, pattern, or texture to your wardrobe mix. Shop for jackets that complement your suit bottoms. This will give your wardrobe more mileage. If in doubt about mixing things up, a safe bet is to wear all black as a base.

Black = Sophisticated, urban. It's the most versatile.

Navy = Classic but difficult to match with other shades of navy.

Gray = Serious business.

Beige = Sleek, skillful, and friendly.

Red = Powerful.

Fabric:

Year round: Lightweight wool, worsted wool, and wool crepe.

Summer: Cotton blends, seersucker, featherweight wool, linen blends.

Fall and winter: Wool, wool blends, cashmere, corduroy, gabardine, tweed, suede, velvet.

Pattern: Solid, pinstripe, plaid, tweed, houndstooth.

SHOP SMART: SHIRTS

A change of shirt will change your look. Your closet should contain about at least five tops. Be sure to buy colors or patterns that complement your suit wardrobe and look appropriate on their own.

- Shirt sleeves should hit the base of the thumb, and extend about a half an inch beyond the sleeve of the jacket.
- There should be enough room in sleeves so you can move your arms comfortably, but not too much that sleeves get bunched up when worn with suit jacket.
- When buttoned up, you should be able to breathe comfortably and there should be no hint of your undergarments or nipples.
- Straight hem: Can be worn untucked in casual environment.
- Shirttail: Must be tucked in.
- Fitted: Crisp and clean, feminine style.
- Rounded collar: Delicate, traditional.
- Spread collar: Best worn outside jacket for splash of style.
- Button-down collar: Man-inspired,

down-to-business, sporty.
- Collarless: Creative, independent.

Color:

Cream = Sophisticated, feminine, approachable.

White = Crisp, classic, down-to-business; wardrobe basic.

Black = Sharp, powerful, assertive.

Monochromatic (to match your suit) = Clean, contemporary, elegant.

Fabric: Those with stretch add comfort.

- Cotton: Clean, crisp.
- Silk: Formal, conservative, dressy.
- Jersey: Easy upkeep, comfortable.

SHOP SMART: KNIT TOPS

Knits can introduce color and texture, and when worn as a sweater set provide a feminine alternative to a suit jacket.

The lighter the weight the more sophisticated the knit, but beware of sheerness, which is never right in the workplace.

Quality is determined by how pure the yarn is and how tight the garment is knitted (gauge). The tighter the knit, the higher the gauge. A one-ply sweater (ply indicates weight) will be a lighter weight, but tighter-knit than a two-ply sweater. An eight-ply knit is very heavy and loosely knit, and more sporty than a one- or two-ply knit. The lighter the weight, the more likely a knit is to shrink, so dry-clean only. Lighter shades take less dye so are softer in feel than darker colors, which use stronger dye.

Fit: Should be fitted, but not tight; too baggy can look sloppy.

- Everything about a turtleneck depends on its fit. Anything oversized or baggy is too casual for the office.

Texture:

- One-ply cashmere is light and more versatile than thicker plies.
- A flat knit is dressier and more versatile than a ribbed one. Worn under a suit jacket, however, the ribbed knit creates a tailored, sporty look.

Fabrics: A top quality merino wool or cotton knit is superior to a poor quality cashmere, which will easily pill and droop.

Color: A sweater is a perfect way to add a dash of color to a neutral suit, whether the season's trendy shade or one that has always suited you.

Smart Options:

Twinset = Classic, feminine.

The black turtleneck = Edgy, urban. Has attitude.

V-neck = Preppy, casual.

SHOP SMART: SKIRTS

A straight, black, knee-length skirt in lightweight wool with a clean waist—no belt loops—is acceptable in even the most conservative settings. It is slimming, can easily mix with other wardrobe items, and can dress up or down.

Fit:

- A slender heel keeps a knee-length skirt from looking overly sensible (aka dowdy).
- A fuller skirt looks best with a fitted top and flatters most body types (though they may overwhelm someone short or thin-boned).
- Straight = To the point, classic, smart.
- A-line = Sensible, friendly.
- Bias-cut = Dressy, sexy.
- Pleated = Youthful, flirty.

Fabric: Should not be heavy or stiff but have a soft drape.

- Lightweight wool: Seasonless, versatile, can be paired with any other texture.

- Jersey: Lightweight stretch fabric best for spring, summer, and early fall.
- Cotton (with stretch): Ideal for spring, summer, and early fall.
- Silk: A more dressed-up look, appropriate for spring and fall.
- Knit: Least versatile option (its extreme texture is limiting and often unflattering). Both light and heavier weaves are acceptable. Best to purchase with a matching top.

SHOP SMART: PANTS

Fit: Use a three-way mirror. If you have a panty line, invest in a thong. Try on pants with the shoes you plan to wear with them to ensure they break softly on top of your shoes. If you are short, avoid cuffs—the longer line extends the leg visually. Avoid pants that tug against tummy or thighs—try a cut with pleats, a fuller leg, or fabric that drapes. If a waistband is causing waist flab, look for a lower cut waist, avoid belts, or wear with tops that are just loose enough to camouflage. Pockets should lie flat, pleats should not pull. Tailors can remove troublesome or visible pockets. Fabric should drape smoothly over the hips to the floor, without pulling or bagging. A fabric that has stretch can make pants more comfortable, fit the body better, and help pants keep their shape.

Color:

Black = Power. The most versatile and flattering.

Gray flannel = Classic, polished, formal.

Beige = Elegant, sophisticated, warm.

Khaki = Creative, laid back, independent.

Smart Options:

Pleated = Sophisticated, classic.

Flat front = Versatile, clean, flattering.

Cuffed = Conservative.

Uncuffed = Minimalist, utilitarian, versatile.

Classic waist = Dressy, capable.

Straight leg = Sleek and fleet.

Not So Smart Options:

Wide leg = Artsy, urban, overly voluminous, inappropriate.

Pegged leg = Rarely flattering.

Flared leg = Hip, trendy. Not office appropriate.

Capri = Carefree. Not office appropriate.

Low waist = Relaxed but raring to go, modern, not office appropriate.

Fabric:

Year round: Lightweight wool, worsted wool, tropical wool, wool crepe. Denim, only if office appropriate.

Summer: Lightweight cotton, cotton blends, lightweight wool.

Fall and winter: Wool, wool blends, corduroy, flannel, gabardine, tweed, suede, velvet.

SHOP SMART: BELTS

If a belt fit is too big or too small, don't throw it away. A shoe repairman can often add extra holes to accommodate.

Color: Black, brown. Should match shoes, unless you choose a bright color.

Texture: Minimal. No studs, rhinestones, or other elaborate decorations. Patent leather finish or interesting texture (alligator) are acceptable.

Buckle: Simple, not overly large or ornate. Choose covered leather (most versatile) or metal (gold or silver).

Width: Standard belt width is one inch, though size must accommodate particular pant or skirt style.

SHOP SMART: TOTES, BRIEFCASES

A tote is practical and appropriate for both formal and more relaxed business environments. Black is versatile and doesn't show dirt. Leather is ideal for quality, professionalism, and longevity. Inner compartments facilitate organization. Size must accommodate legal papers and ideally a laptop, but not be overly big: It will look like you are being overwhelmed by work, especially if you are petite—and may be a stress on your back or shoulders.

SHOP SMART: BAGS AND SHOES

BAGS

For optimum organization, an everyday handbag should always be stocked with stashable compartments. It should also zip, snap, or latch shut for safety and for one-step concealment of that rare disorganized moment. A smaller handbag—a clutch, perhaps—that fits into a larger one can come in handy for lunches or evening events where a tote or briefcase might seem unwieldy.

Color:

Camel = Relaxed, understated luxury.

Cordovan = Rich, elegant.

Brown = Conservative, classic.

Beige = Crisp, sophisticated.

Black patent = Snappy, dressy in spring and summer.

SHOES

- If you don't have them—midheight black evening pumps—it's time. For winter, consider boots.

- Buy the best everyday shoes you can. Try to have two pairs to alternate each day, allowing each pair to breathe and dry out.

SHOP SMART: DRESSES

A dress is one-stop dressing. Whether worn with a jacket or without, a dress brings feminine—and professional—flair to a work closet. In a solid color it is easier to transform with accessories than one in a pattern. Large patterns will make you appear larger than small subtle patterns, and is less business appropriate. If you are wide in the middle avoid waistlines.

SHOP SMART: SCARVES

Scarves expand your wardrobe and provide a quick change to an outfit. They brighten up plain neutrals with color or pattern, help soften a professional look, enhance your face, and can draw attention away from your neck or cleavage.

Smart Options:

- 36" square silk: classic, most versatile, and most popular in a print.
- 12" x 48" oblong silk scarf.
- A hand-rolled edge is luxurious.
- A fringe trim is sportif.

Fabric:

- Silk = Classic, elegant.
- Cotton = Casual, summery.
- Chiffon = Feminine, flirty.
- Fine lightweight wool = Warm, confident.

How to Wear It:

- A scarf should incorporate the color accents of your wardrobe and flatter your coloring as it will usually be placed near your face.
- A scarf should look soft and natural, not stiff or overproduced.
- Choose lightweight, not bulky, and avoid wearing any style that requires frequent adjusting.
- Avoid the appearance of being engulfed by your scarf.
- Don't let a long scarf hang below your waist. It appears messy, dowdy, and shortens your leg line.

- Pocket squares (16"–18") add a bit of flourish to a suit jacket. Place softly by picking up in the middle of square, and fold bottom up slightly to shorten head. Tuck into jacket breast pocket, so ends softly peak out of pocket about 1-1½".

SHOP SMART: RAINCOAT

Along with its utilitarian duties, the raincoat must reflect a level of professionalism on par with the rest of your wardrobe. Avoid the superfluous conceit of a hood.

Most Versatile Style: Black raincoat with zip-out lining says classic, competent, practical. It can be dressy or casual.

Fabric:

- Water resistant: Can withstand small amounts of moisture.
- Waterproof: Can resist all weather.
- Shiny plastic: Avoid.
- Matte nylon (or nylon blend): Gives sophisticated urban look.
- Microfiber or techno blend: Newest development, most practical. Very lightweight, which makes it easy to pack and seasonless.

SHOP SMART: COATS

With its uniformlike decorum and sweep of fabric, a coat can be a dramatic power accessory and, depending on color and details, reflect your personality and taste. Like the raincoat, a coat must be as polished and professional as the rest of your business wardrobe.

- Choose a coat that has an easy fit; nothing too formal, fitted, or uptight. It must fit well over suit.
- Length, color, and silhouette must be compatible with the palette and style of the clothes you wear underneath.
- Shoulders should fit squarely, with the seams reaching the outer edge of the shoulder. A wider fit means the coat is too big.
- Avoid extreme, overly wide shoulders. Shoulder pads should be minimal.
- Armholes should allow movement.
- The lining should fall freely inside the garment but not hang beneath the hemline.
- Shop for classic cuts in late January, when coats go on sale.
- Buy the best fabric you can afford.
- Sleeves should reach to the top of the thumb.
- Avoid excess details such as extra buttons, epaulets, and buckles.

Top Options: Melton (strong, sturdy wool with great body), cashmere, wool blends.

SHOP SMART: MATERNITY

Just because you're pregnant, there is no reason not to feel good about the way you look as your body transforms over nine months. The right clothes should give you delight when you get dressed each morning. Look at this as an opportunity to create a brand-new professional wardrobe.

- A couple of suits will get you through your pregnancy—the more they can be mixed and matched, the less bored you'll get.
- Your body temperature will heat up so dress in seasonless fabrics and in layers.
- Wear clothes close to the body—it's more flattering than big and baggy. But avoid anything tight. A protruding belly button is unprofessional.
- Solid-colored clothes are more versatile than prints. Add pattern through accessories.
- Buy black. It's a wardrobe stretcher and it's slimming.
- Buy more tops than bottoms—it's the quickest and cheapest way to change a look.
- If your legs are an asset, draw attention to them by wearing skirts.
- Your feet may swell and go up in size, so buy comfortable shoes, but not expensive ones as you probably won't need them after the baby is born.
- Support hose or tights are available in maternity sizes.

Work Wardrobe

Mission accomplished. You got the job. The next step: To build a work wardrobe that works for you. This is accomplished by: 1. Expanding the number of suits in your closet and 2. Knowing which items to choose to create a myriad of different looks. That can mean a stash of crisp shirts, a perfect A-line skirt; even belts, scarves, and shoes that can jump-start a look. What follows is a two-year game plan that will guide you through a simple, focused closet expansion.

"You can't just sit there and wait for people to give you that golden dream. You've got to get out there and make it happen for yourself."

DIANA ROSS

DOES MY WARDROBE MEAN BUSINESS?

Suits First...

Four Essential Suits. Expanding your closet from one suit to four—neutral colors, seasonless fabrics—dramatically expands your wardrobe possibilities. Choose wisely. Each piece can be worn in several ways to create at least 32 different looks. That's wardrobe economics.

GRAY SUIT

BEIGE SUIT

Wardrobe Follows

Black+Color

A black suit is sleek, sophisticated, and, no matter what the situation, appropriate. (It's also slimming, virtually immune to dirt, and, to the less-than-sure dresser, safe.) Black mixes effortlessly with accessories of all colors and textures, each one giving the simple silhouette a different identity.

BAGS
Burgundy tote = Worldly, imaginative.
Camel tote = Timeless.
Black patent tote = Polished.

SHOES
Burgundy sling backs = Feminine, functional.
Black pumps = Elegant, sleek.

COLOR BASICS

Stark neutral colors, including the strong monochromatic look, give the classic black suit extra edge.

PRIMARY SHIRTS
Cream = Sophisticated.
White = Classic.
Black = Edgy.

SEASONAL COLORS

Trade the cashmere turtleneck for a pastel linen blouse, and the black suit goes from winterized to screaming spring.

FALL/WINTER OPTIONS
Red cotton pique shirt = Bold.
Camel turtleneck = Classic.
Gray sweater = Industrious.
Houndstooth blouse = Refined.

SPRING/SUMMER OPTIONS
Fuchsia knit = Dynamic.
Mint green cotton = Pensive.
Sky blue linen = Amiable.

HOSIERY
Opaque black = Workaday.
Sheer black = Dressy, sexy. Best worn at night.
Nude = Conservative.
Each of these colors can be worn with the shoes shown here.

Gray+Color

Polished, presentable, and subtle, a gray suit is a workaday staple. Browns and black are classic pairings with shades of gray. And any color is compatible with it, bringing a welcome jolt. Mixing tweeds and checks with gray can give the subdued hue an added richness and depth.

BAGS AND SHOES
Monochromatic tones: Elegant, sophisticated.
With black: Urban, sleek.
With brown: Efficient, relaxed.

COLOR BASICS

Neutral colors add to a gray suit's subdued sophistication. How to keep gray-on-gray from being ho-hum? Make it flashy satin.

PRIMARY SHIRTS
Gray satin = Dramatic.
White = Conscientious.
Black = Contemplative, cool.

SEASONAL COLORS

Ever agreeable, gray can go with anything from a classic blue oxford to playful pink satin.

FALL/WINTER OPTIONS
Pink satin = Sociable.

SPRING/SUMMER OPTIONS
Striped cotton = Amicable.
Blue oxford = Conservative.
Red cotton knit = Energetic.

HOSIERY
Opaque black = Utilitarian, cosmopolitan. Pair with any of the shoes here.
Sheer black = Dressy. Wear with sling backs or pumps.
Nude = Conservative.

Beige+Color

A beige suit is always sleek and subdued. Far from slimming, however, beige creates an elongated line only when worn monochromatically with similar tones. It's also tricky, but not impossible, to dress up for evening, looking better with pearls, gold, and tortoiseshell jewelry than with silver. But beware: Buff shades tend to be high maintenance, making dirt and wrinkling plain to the naked eye.

BAGS
Brown tote = American heritage.
Black shoulder bag = Business basic.
Beige handbag = Elegant.

SHOES
Brown suede flats = Urban.
Low black pumps = Go-getter.
Low beige pumps = Well-bred.

COLOR BASICS

The minimalism of a beige suit is maximized when paired with neutral hues—black, white, and other shades of beige.

PRIMARY SHIRTS
Monochromatic T-shirt = Uncomplicated.
White shirt = Respectable.
Black shirt = Artsy.

SEASONAL COLORS

With a red corduroy shirt (winter) or candy-colored stripes (spring), beige is a suit for all seasons.

SPRING/SUMMER OPTIONS
Bright stripes = Mischievous.
Pale blue knit = Thoughtful.

FALL/WINTER OPTIONS
Neutral stripes = Refined.
Gray wool knit = Traditional.
Red corduroy = Rugged.

HOSIERY
Opaque black = No-nonsense. Pair with black or brown shoes.
Sheer black = Dressed up. Wear with black or brown shoes.
Nude = Traditional. Appropriate with all shoes here.

Navy+Color

Classic and clean, a navy suit is a kinder, gentler alternative to black that still presents a military-caliber decorum. Navy tends to go with everything except other navies, so buy suit pieces together; don't mix and match. Camel and gray are naturally compatible with it, while a striped crew neck gives it a preppy-nautical air. As for accessories, black tends to dress up a navy suit; brown and beige make it more casual.

BAGS AND SHOES
Burgundy nylon and leather tote = Metropolitan.
Black tote = Practical.
Brown pumps = Sensible.
Low black pumps = Commanding.

COLOR BASICS

Navy looks most corporate paired with a crisp white shirt or another, carefully chosen-to-match navy.

PRIMARY SHIRTS
Navy polo shirt = Efficient.
White shirt = Crisp, conservative.

SEASONAL COLORS

It's perfect with pastels in summer and bright colors in winter; but if considering pairing navy with red, beware of nautical overkill.

SPRING/SUMMER OPTIONS
Pink cotton = Preppy.
Blue linen = Animated.

FALL/WINTER OPTIONS
Red knit = Nautical.
Blue stripes = Upbeat.

HOSIERY
Opaque black = Serious business. Wear with black or brown shoes.
Sheer black = More formal. Wear with black shoes.
Nude = Classic. Wear with black or brown shoes.

CHIC SIMPLE

1 SUIT = 4 OUTFITS

A work wardrobe is built by laying a foundation—a good suit—then adding a variety of pieces to go with it. The trick is mixing those pieces together to create winning outfits. In these pages, classic gray suit separates are shown with items that will maximize their potential.

SUIT JACKET + SKIRT

A tailored suit jacket can be worn with the skirts and pants—and crisp shirts and cool turtlenecks—in your closet, for a dash of instant decorum. Think about texture. If the jacket has a flat, smooth weave, don't pair it with a skirt that's too bulky or flimsy—make sure weights match.

SUIT SKIRT + SWEATER SET

A suit skirt paired with a blouse, sweater, or jacket has a relaxed but professional, feminine feel. Check proportion. A fuller top should be worn with a skinny skirt, and vice versa. If a skirt has belt loops, tuck in the top and wear a belt. Pairing a skirt with a sweater set is pulled together and ladylike.

SUIT JACKET + TURTLENECK

A black turtleneck paired with a suit can convey creative cool (think beat poets of the 50s), while a color can come off as preppy and pristine. Complete the look with accessories that have equal attitude—boots, black opaque hosiery, and a substantial bag balance the attitude of a black turtleneck.

SUIT PANTS + JACKET

Whether worn with a contrasting jacket or a monochromatic blouse, suit pants give an outfit a sleek, on-the-go edge. Paired with a zip-front, collarless jacket, proper suit pants have an instant no-nonsense attitude. Paired with a knit sweater set it is feminine and pulled together.

Wardrobe Enhancers...

The strong stance of a jacket gives a look a sense of unity, contributes color and texture, and adds a dash of respectability to anything from a delicate skirt to denim. A growing collection of jackets will help expand your work wardrobe.

BLAZER
Competent, approachable. Classic, tailored silhouettes— strong shoulders, single- or double-breasted, with a hem that reaches to the bottom of the hip.

CARDIGAN JACKET
On-duty but at ease. Slouchy fit, boxy shape, can be cropped to the waist or extend to the bottom of the hip.

COLOR
A jacket can provide a look with a welcome jolt of color (whereas red, lime green, or lilac pants are rare).

DOUBLE-BREASTED
Highly polished, highly professional. A bit flashier than a single-breasted jacket, with its double row of buttons and its sharply tailored, upward-slashing lapels, it is more formal and imposing. Always wear buttoned up except for either the top or bottom button, which is left unbuttoned.

BLACK JACKET
The most classic, versatile, and authoritative
item of clothing you will own, a black jacket is
a business staple, and the best (cloth-bound)
investment in your career you can make.

Jacket

CHIC SIMPLE

Knit Tops

LONG SLEEVE

TURTLENECK

A turtleneck is a sleek, modern, and slightly relaxed alternative to the corporate board-room look. The most dressy and versatile choice is black. It is edgy, urban, and has attitude. Worn under a suit jacket, it creates a sporty tailored look.

SHORT SLEEVE

SWEATER SET

A cardigan worn over a matching shell or sweater, a sweater set is a soft but polished alternative to a suit jacket. Paired with a pencil skirt or a pair of trousers, a sweater set is feminine and sophisticated.

SLEEVELESS

Skirts

Worn with a jacket, it forms a sharp, hyperfemi-
nine suit. Worn without, it's a classic, polished
alternative to trousers. Your goal: To supplement
your wardrobe with skirts whose length, fit, and
cut easily mix with the suit jackets and other
clothes in your closet. But beware: Depending
on style, a skirt can say sleek and sophisticated
(appropriate) or girly, flirty, or dowdy (inappropriate). Choose a midheight, block-heeled
pump with opaque or semiopaque hosiery or a
high-heeled classic pump that should be worn
with sheer, semiopaque, or opaque hose. Or
choose nude, which is the most conservative.

FIRST PURCHASE

A straight, black, knee-length skirt in lightweight wool with a clean waist—no belt
loops—is acceptable even in the most
conservative settings. Bonus: It is slimming,
can easily mix with other wardrobe items,
and with a change of accessories can dress
up or down with ease.

KNEE = SERIOUS BUSINESS

MIDCALF = PROFESSIONAL, UNASSUMING

ANKLE = ARTSY, SLINKY, LAID-BACK

Pants

The archetypal symbol of a woman in charge, pants have become a sartorial standard in any business wardrobe. Properly chosen and well tailored, they provide a relaxed and practical alternative to a dress or skirt. A few extra pairs of pants can expand a wardrobe exponentially. But pants vary greatly in style. Choosing silhouettes and fabrics that are professional and flattering is key. In some conservative corporate environments pants are considered inappropriate for women. If you work in such a setting, stick with a skirt until you determine the exact dress code.

BLACK PANTS
Versatile, seasonless, flattering. Black pants in a year-round fabric—light or midweight wool—can be worn with just about anything else in your closet.

PLEATED, CUFFED TROUSERS
Classic, put together. Wear with a tailored shirt or pretty blouse— with or without a jacket.

A drop waistline should never bare any skin at work.

Belt loops require a belt.

FLAT-FRONT PANTS
Trim, sleek, together. Beige pants are elegant and friendly, when worn with a black top and black accessories. It looks softer and more feminine when you mix with colors such as pale blue or white.

A pleated front, a wider leg, and the gentle drape of fabric.

KHAKIS
Thanks to the dot-com crew, in very laid-back offices khakis are key. Add decorum through what they're paired with: A blazer or sweater set, polished boots or shoes, good accessories. Dress them up. Don't let them dress you down.

* A fabric that has stretch can make pants more comfortable, fit the body better, and keep their shape.

Dress

More feminine than a suit, if less versatile, a dress can be a woman's secret weapon: It eliminates the time and bother of mixing and matching separates.

FIRST PURCHASE

A black dress can be at once both formal and informal depending on the cut, fabric, and the shoes and bag you choose to wear with it. Bonus: It slims the body, conceals imperfect tailoring, and brings focus to your face, which is where you want it at work.

SHOES AND HOSIERY
Midheight, block-heeled pump. High-heeled classic pump. Pair midheight pump with opaque or semiopaque hosiery; high-heeled pump with sheer, semiopaque, or opaque. Or choose nude (especially for dress evenings).

DRESS SUIT
For business days that extend into evenings out, a dress under a matching jacket can go from suit-like to festive— simply toss the jacket.

SILHOUETTE	DEFINITION	WHAT IT SAYS
Dress Suit	Matching dress and blazer	Sophisticated, quiet confidence
Sheath Dress	Straight, loose-fitting column	Traditional, hardworking
Shirt Dress	Button-front, inspired by mens' shirts	Feminine, flexible, flirty
Wrap Dress	Wraparound V-neck, self-tying	Competent, refined
Knit Dress	Woven fabric	Conservative, old-world elegance

BUSINESS
Denim

Once the exclusive domain of miners, college coeds, and weekend warriors, denim has shed its rugged reputation to become a civilized member of liberal workplaces. Given a suitably casual office, denim may be appropriate worn with its pulled-together counterpart—a tailored jacket or sweater set. But wear with caution! In order to pass at work, the fabric must be well chosen, in good condition, and fit perfectly. In an office setting, only one item of clothing within an outfit should be denim. Balance it with refined, high-quality counterparts (i.e., jackets, skirts, etc.).

COLOR
The darker the dressier.

LENGTH
Skirt to or just below the knee.

SKIRT
Don't go casual with the top. Balance denim with a crisp, clean button-down shirt, tailored business blazer, or a sweater set for a pulled-together, casual look.

JACKET

A jacket gives denim instant respectability.

FIT

Be mindful of fit around the
hips. Too tight looks suggestive.
Too baggy looks careless.
Some stretch helps denim
keep its shape.

CRISP AND CLEAN

No wrinkling or fraying.
Consider dry-cleaning
or ironing office denim.
As for color: Black or
dark blue. No fading.

STRAIGHT LEG

Choose a straight
or tapered leg.
No flares.

Shoes and Bags

Functional and, let's face it, fun, accessories provide a welcome expression of personal style that can make women giddy. They're also a quick, affordable fix when refreshing your business wardrobe each season. A new shoe or bag and the whole look is new.

SMART OPTIONS:

- A smaller handbag—a clutch, perhaps—that fits into a larger one can come in handy for lunches or evening events where a tote or briefcase might seem unwieldy.
- If you have not yet opted for the classic black pump that also works for dressier evening functions, put it high on your shopping list.

Tote

TOTE DIMENSIONS
10 3/4" H x 16 1/2" W x 3 1/2" D

Briefcase

As your career progresses, work takes up more and more of your everyday life—and wardrobe. You'll need a bag—either a tote or a briefcase—that looks appropriate, and that can accommodate files, a laptop, official documents, and meeting notes.

BRIEFCASE DIMENSIONS
10 3/4" H x 14 1/2" W x 3 3/4" D

Belts

A belt is required whenever belt loops are present. The converse is also true: In the absence of belt loops, a belt is rarely appropriate. Belts keep a look pulled together and, as such, should be discreet, versatile, and of good quality. Save the fashion statements for after hours.

WIDTH
Standard is one inch, though size must accommodate belt loops on your suit, skirt, or pants.

Scarves

Tied around the neck or draped over the shoulders, a scarf can add a feminine flourish to a business look, and breathe new life into clothes. A scarf can brighten a plain suit with a splash of color or pattern and draw attention to your face.

FOR A SMART PULLED-TOGETHER LOOK THAT ELIMINATES THE NEED FOR A NECKLACE:

1. Fold a square scarf into an oblong by folding corners in and into fourths.

2. Place around the neck and flip one end over the other in front.

3. Bring both ends around the back of your neck and tie in a simple knot.

4. This is the view from the back.

5. This is the view from the front.

Raincoat

A classic raincoat is indispensable. Along with its utilitarian duties, at times it will be the first and last impression you make—literally. The right raincoat can also serve you on crisp, dry days, allowing you to delay purchasing a wool coat until your budget allows.

FIRST PURCHASE

Choose a trench or balmacaan (single-breasted with raglan sleeves) in a cotton or wool gabardine, ideally with a zip-out microfiber lining. Be sure the cut is full enough to fit comfortably over your suits and long enough to cover their skirts.

THE BURBERRY CLASSIC

In 1856, Thomas Burberry, the British sportswear manufacturer, created the gabardine trench, which went on to serve as uniform for nineteenth-century adventurers, World War I men-in-the-trenches, sleuths, spies, and generations of professionals. Burberry's classic trench continues to be a best-seller for men and women, having sold more than a million since 1917.

BUTTON-DOWN EPAULET
Once used to secure a rifle over the shoulder; today, a civilized detail.

STORM FLAP
Buttons over the chest.

BUCKLED CUFF
Staves off the wind.

BREATHABLE FABRIC
As conceived by British sportswear manufacturer Thomas Burberry, the trench coat is made of tight weaves of cotton and wool (which he dubbed gabardine) that allow air to pass through them, alleviating the drenching effect of a mackintosh.

CLOTH BELT
Usually worn tied (in front or back), not buckled, but should never be left dangling.

WOOL LINING
Insulation against the cold. Removable a must.

LENGTH
Be sure trench is longer than your skirt suits.

COLOR
Khaki is classic; black is a new classic.

UMBRELLA

Unless you are looking for the flourish of a full-sized, formal umbrella, a compact travel size makes the most sense for business. You can stash it in your tote for iffy days and pack it in your suitcase when on the road. Black is subdued and goes with everything.

Cold Weather
NECESSITIES

With its uniformlike
decorum and
sweep of fabric,
a coat can be
a dramatic
power accessory.
Over time, you will
build a wardrobe
of them, but your initial
purchase should be practical,
polished, and professional.

WINTER SCARF
Stylish, sensible. A bright color,
or neutral—in wool, a wool
blend, or cashmere—that is
not overly long or large, or an
extremely thick weave.

WOOL HAT

Well-equipped. Black, weatherproof fabric in a classic shape.

GLOVES

Polished, prepared. Black leather gloves should be snug and, for sufficient warmth, lined.

WEATHERPROOF BOOTS

Elegant, together. Black, treated leather with a heel that won't skid when it hits a puddle.

COAT

Select a good wool coat with clean lines that is long and roomy enough to accommodate your suit comfortably. Black is the most versatile, looking great day or night, and slow to show dirt. Camel and navy are suitable for day. Red is a powerful declaration of professional and personal style. Choose compatible cold-weather accessories: Hat, scarf, gloves, and boots.

Work Wardrobe:

Your maternity clothes should be a capsule version of your business wardrobe. That means professional, polished clothes—albeit in larger sizes with some extra stretch here and there—that give you delight when you get dressed in the morning.

TOPS
Wear a body-skimming base layer—T-shirt, camisole, fitted sweater—under a looser shirt and/or jacket or cardigan.

REMIX
For variety, buy more tops (in different colors) to mix and match with a small number of bottoms.

PANTS
Elasticized waist and pants with stretch are maternity saviors.

COLOR
Buy solid-colored clothes; they're more versatile than prints. Add pattern through accessories.

FIT
Wear clothes close to the body—it's more flattering than big and baggy. However, the trend of skin-tight fit is inappropriate at work.

SHOES
Don't spend a lot of money on shoes to accommodate your changing foot size. Buy cheap. You may never wear them again.

Maternity

VERSATILITY

A simple black dress will take you everywhere—from a business lunch to a wedding.

DETAILS

To avoid head-to-toe volume, make sure the shirt is not overly large and that pants are properly hemmed and taper in the leg.

HOSIERY

Buy support hose or tights to reduce leg swelling—they're available in maternity sizes.

CHIC SIMPLE

CLOSET work wardrobe

You have established your closet as your ally in your climb up the ladder. Like your impressive Rolodex, your handy filing system, and your flair with clients, it is another career tool you can always rely on and one of the factors that makes you uniquely spectacular at the job you do.

CLOSET UPDATE

Along with four neutral suits, you have tops to go with them—in styles, colors, and fabrics to suit any season, circumstance, or mood; shoes and handbags that are appropriate to the outfit and the occasion; and other accessories that have you prepared for any business (or weather) phenomenon that comes your way. And all without purchasing unnecessarily large amounts of clothes. Your closet, like your desk, is stocked with the supplies that you need. What you don't see you won't wear, so organizing your closet is key, as well as not overstuffing it. It's also easier to mix and match things at a glance. Keep professional clothes together to get a quick overview of your choices, and hang like things together, then sort by color. Late summer and late winter is the best time to assess your professional wardrobe for the upcoming season. Clean, then store off-season clothes and accessories.

CLOTHES CHECK

- Check color combinations (especially hosiery) in natural lighting before leaving home.
- If a garment needs repair, take to tailor immediately.
- Check your shoes. Worn ones can bring down your look.
- Keep silver jewelry clean.
- Have all pieces of a suit cleaned together to avoid eventual color or sheen mismatch.
- Don't dry-clean clothes frequently—it's hard on clothes.

CHANGE OF LIFE

Dear Kim and jeff,
I'm getting ready for some major changes in my workplace. I'm going
from being a college counselor in New York to being a dean of a university
in California. How do I make the wardrobe change to reflect this new
position of authority without breaking the bank? And should I make some
changes in my wardrobe based on the move to California? After all, living
in New York has meant living in black.
—Dean-to-Be

Dear Dean-to-Be,
You're right, California is different from New York; however, a dean is
a very visible leadership position, and a suit best projects professional
authority. Invest in a good one, then change its look by a change in shirt,
shoes, or by wearing different silk scarves around your neck. Consider
purchasing a power watch. It's a practical piece of jewelry that will signal
success; and you will enjoy it daily.

—Kim and jeff

Get Better Job **3**

Power Wardrobe

Power is an elusive pursuit. There is always someone with a bigger cubicle, a brighter office, a better company, a more decked-out jet. The truth is, success comes not from the achievement of power but from the joy of the process, from taking pleasure in work and in doing it well. Your clothes should signal that you are unmistakably worthy of your current status—and/or ready to take the next step. To get that message across best, make sure your clothes, like your actions, are direct, consistent, and, yes, smart. Dress smart.

Clothes Confidence
—Dressing Like You Mean It

SCHLEPLESS
Men have long equated power with carrying less—the higher the rung on the ladder, the thinner the attaché, the smaller the briefcase. Women often find it difficult to quit schlepping. Invest in a smaller bag, and the rest will follow.

No matter how confident you are that you have arrived, you are never absolved from projecting an image of power. After all, there is always someone higher up to impress. And looking like you deserve it can protect the authority you have and pave the way for a smooth move up to acquire more. Achieving a power-worthy look is an ongoing process. It requires a little self-examination and a lot of discrimination—the ability to choose clothes that command respect, ooze quality, and reflect a sense of authority that is uniquely suitable to you.

AUTHORITY DRESSING

"I used to wear leggings to work every day," says HarperCollins CEO, Jane Friedman. "But when I became CEO, they looked too unimportant. It didn't look like I was giving credence to my own position. Now, I get my hair done twice a week, I have manicures every week, and I do think more about what I'm putting on."

When in a leadership role, your job is to make an impact. Whether you're sending out a memo or breezing down the hall for a meeting, you must convey confidence, integrity, quality, authority, and power.

Your clothes can help you do that by sending a clear, consistent message that solidifies your identity and is compatible with your personality and work philosophies. What does this mean in terms of your closet? In general, everything needs an upgrade. Suits should be better quality. Accessories should be chosen with more discretion.

In terms of specifics, looks that signal authority will vary depend-ing on the industry, the office, and the individual. Your job is to fine-tune your wardrobe and formulate a uniform that makes you look and feel powerful. If you work in a creative office, it might be a minimalist look with a dash of fashion that signals authority: A suede skirt, boots, and a turtleneck or black pants, a crisp white shirt, and a leather blazer. If you work in banking, authority might come from giving your suit wardrobe an upgrade in quality and buying one or two pairs of really good shoes and bags.

THE POWER OF QUALITY

"I tend to buy good things, investments, and keep them," says *Travel & Leisure* editor in chief, Nancy Novogrod. "It's not that I'm being frivolous. I feel it's my responsibility, in my position, to buy nice clothing and to look a certain way."

Publisher Judith Regan has a similar philosophy about dressing for a position of power: "My style hasn't changed; my clothes just get better as I get richer—the tailoring gets richer, the fabric gets richer."

An item of high quality is beautifully made, with utter integrity, of the highest caliber materials available: A cashmere sweater, a Rolex watch, a Jaguar. Quality is the first and primary indicator of a commanding presence. If you think and act with discretion, you will choose your clothes with discretion, too. At this stage of the game, you can afford it. People will be looking for it. It's not an extravagance. It's a requirement.

Learn to recognize quality in its various forms. Go to Tiffany. Wander through Hermès. Take a wine-tasting class. Browse designer boutiques or the designer floor of a department store, and try on suits by Giorgio Armani, Calvin Klein, Donna Karan. What's the difference between these suits and the ones you are accustomed to wearing? Look at the waistband. The finished seams. The lining. Notice the texture of the fabric, the weightiness of it, the drape, the feel.

PALETTE POWER

"Brown is my black," says News Corporation's Anthea Disney. "Most of my clothes are brown and, just to live dangerously, taupe. It suits my coloring. I have brown hair and brown eyes and fairly tannish skin. And a lot of people can't wear brown, so it's a little differentiator."

Settling on a distinct color palette simplifies shopping and dress-

3. Get Better Job

POWER OF CONTRADICTION
Fine fabric, sharp, architectural lines—these are the first images that come to mind as symbolic of dressing with authority. In today's work world, women don't need linebacker shoulderpads to command respect—a monochromatic palette with soft fluid lines might make just the statement. It's the genuine confidence that comes through the clothes that matters, not the appearance of confidence that's stitched into them.

ing, makes a strong statement, and gives you an impossible-to-miss mark of individuality. Among the colors that command authority: Pale neutrals (cream, beige), red, black, white, blues, and pastels when attached to the oomph of a suit.

Besides, in a serious business setting, as former congresswoman Pat Schroeder discovered while working on the floor of the House, color can be a rare, and very welcome, glimmer of brilliance:

"When I was on the floor, there would be 450 dark suits, so I wondered, what's the one thing I can do? I decided to put a little color in the place. My constituents were sitting up in the balcony; they're more apt to see me. If the camera pans, I'm more visible."

A CUT ABOVE, WHEN DIFFERENT WORKS

Following the pack is not always mandatory. When Pat Schroeder was photographed with the elected congresswomen for the cover of the *New York Times Magazine* in 1977, she was the only one not sporting "a little suit and a little bow tie. I'm not a male wannabe," she says. "And that's what that said to me. I couldn't do it." Instead, she wore a dress. Guess which of those congresswomen ended up running for president?

This is who can get away with setting their own dress code: People in very creative industries. People who work for themselves (Condé Nast owner Si Newhouse is famous for his gray sweatshirts). People in extra–laid-back, dress-code-free offices. People who answer to the title "boss" (publisher Sonny Mehta is famous for wearing a suit and tie one day, a T-shirt and leather sandals the next), and people who are off-the-charts good at their jobs and, as such, above it all.

If you work with someone who eschews the dress code, think twice before emulating his or her fashion MO. That option may not apply to you. But if it does…

Look the Part, Get the Part
—Dressing for Your New Position

DRESSING FOR YOUR NEXT POSITION

Power dressing means looking ahead, knowing the path you want to take, and preparing yourself for it in every way. You wouldn't expect to be hired for a job and then acquire the skills necessary to do it. The same is true for your look: You have to look the part before anyone is going to give it to you. The higher you rise, the more subtle the cues. No one is going to run the risk of "We'll see if he's up to it or ends up looking the part." You have to look and act your future now. Dress for tomorrow. Act as though you've already reached your goals and you're halfway there.

HOW TO LOOK "MORE":

Professional: Wear a suit. If you already wear a suit, upgrade your suit—better fabric, better tailoring. Choose details that instantly signal polish and decorum, such as sleek high heels, a crisp, collared shirt, or pearls. Other symbols of corporate credibility: Dark colors and immaculate grooming, and anything that suggests utter organization, whether it's a Palm (instead of a wrinkled Filofax) or an impossibly small handbag.

Responsible/Reliable: Make sure every detail is attended to. Have a great haircut. Get a manicure. Organize the elements in your handbag. Have your shoes polished.

Management-worthy: Good management is a balance between

approachability and authority. Cultivate a refined mix of the two styles by giving a laid-back look a single splash of authority. For a softer corporate look, wear a suede jacket with a pencil skirt and high heels. Or choose a relaxed beige suit—khakis with a sleek suit jacket.

Independent: Take a risk. Deviate from the norm. If your colleagues are stuck in a middle-of-the-road business appropriate rut, wear a suit. Wear it with a colorful blouse. If you're surrounded by suits, wear yours with a denim shirt. Or red stilettos. If you wear glasses, choose frames that express your style. If you don't wear glasses, consider getting a pair as a fashion statement.

Open: Unbutton your shirt collar a little. Don't lacquer every hair in place with spray. Try a sweater set in place of a suit jacket. Every once in a while, toss your outfit a curve—wear a pin that has personal meaning or a pair of feminine sling backs.

Creative: Express a little personal style. Wear a scarf in your hair. Test drive the latest trendy shoes. Try the season's key color—lime green, gypsy purple. Wear a necklace, bracelet, or earrings that you love. Tamper with the corporate dress code.

Authoritative: Upgrade your suits. Upgrade your shoes, your handbag, and your coat—fine fabric and expert handiwork indicate serious business. Wear details that signal power and command, such as pinstripes or the color red. Invest in a high-quality, signature accessory, like a Hermès scarf or a designer handbag.

Friendly: Wear color. Dress with a sense of humor. Wear a blouse with a polka-dot, floral print, or in a whimsical color. Tie a silk scarf loosely around your neck.

Communicative/Compassionate: Loosen up. Choose knits over tailoring, sweaters in place of jackets. Try the softness of a skirt instead of the armor of a pantsuit. Be feminine—wear a dress, a pretty blouse, colors that are soft instead of dark.

LITTLE THINGS: ACCESSORIES THAT WORK FOR YOU

Going from looking like one of the pack to its leader can often be achieved with a quick change of an accessory. If it's a trend-related industry, buy a fashionable handbag or shoes. If it's law, real estate, or a corporate environment, investigate high-quality briefcases, pens, or agendas. If you frequently entertain clients, you might consider a high-quality designer wallet. In any high-end business, a high-end watch sig-

IMAGE MAKERS
When you gain control of your image, you gain control of your life.

nals success and power. Investing in an item or two that signals serious business for your particular situation will make you look and feel at the top of your game.

CONSISTENCY = CREDIBILITY

When Al Gore was running for president, he traded his ceremonious gray suits for relaxed pleated pants, tossed his starched shirts for the hip Henleys being worn at trendy bars, and occasionally was spotted in cowboy boots. "He suddenly went from Mr. Wooden to this Mr. Cool, Mr. Yuppie look, out of the blue. It was a PR disaster," says Kathy Ardleigh, who spent decades consulting politicians on their public image and currently oversees the issue at Fox TV. "They were trying to change his persona through his outfit. And you know what? When people are uncomfortable, it shows. You can tweak someone's look but you can't change it dramatically."

Clothes can help highlight existing character traits—a suit can bring to light your go-getter side; high heels sharpen those killer instincts—but they cannot, costumelike, create an entirely different you. Besides, if you're in a job where the required dress code is downright alien, the culture you've entered into may not be one for you.

Laura Bush, on the other hand, retained the very same look she had as wife of the governor of Texas when she became first lady of the United States. "I like the fact that she's confident enough in herself not to feel she has to make major and drastic changes," Ardleigh says.

The moral: Dress the part, but as it applies to you. Be true to yourself and your authenticity will show.

3. Get Better Job

Power Dressing

UNIFORM STYLE: WRITING YOUR OWN DRESS CODE

If your unique talents have propelled you to a level of status, where you're free to create a dress code that's unique to you, break rules. Push boundaries. But be aware that you are sending a visual signal to those who work for you that they too may stretch the rules.

UNIFORM DECISIONS

On day one of your career, you probably had one suit, one color, one signature look. Next came a career full of wardrobe experimentation, fluctuation, and accumulation (aka closet adolescence). Now the goal is to pare back down to one signature look again: Ideally one suit, silhouette, and a consistent color palette that acts as backdrop for as singular a uniform as you can stand. The more clarity and precision your look has, the stronger its impact—and the more unforgettable your presence.

SIGNATURE PIECES

Agent Binky Urban wears all beige with personal flair. Britney Spears built her reputation while baring her torso. And the world's fashion figures have all had distinct trademarks: Carrie Donovan had her over-sized glasses; *Vogue* editor Anna Wintour, her immaculate (and unmissable) bob.

If there's a distinct detail that naturally evolves out of your style, consider emphasizing it as your signature: Perhaps it's a color or designer you wear without fail. Maybe you have an heirloom locket or unique jewelry from a designer you admire. If you gravitate to scarves, consider collecting Hermès. If you're a classicist, perhaps your signature is pearls. Be creative. Think of the women whose looks you admire— what makes their looks memorable?

DETAILS TO CONSIDER

Silhouette: Choose a silhouette (or two) that suits you. Stick to double-breasted suits. Or pencil skirts with sweater sets. This silhouette will be the backdrop to every outfit you put on.

Color: Decide on a color palette for visual distinction. Are you more suited to monochromatic black, jewel tones, or pastels? Power red or creams and beiges?

Style: Determine your style and stick with it. Do you prefer classics, clothes with a hip edge, or a combination of the two?

Accessories: It's often these details that make the defining difference.

- Do you reach for a classic Kelly bag, or prefer a new bag each season?
- Do you have a wardrobe of timepieces or are you more confident wearing a Cartier Tank watch each day?

The goal is to be able to compose your wardrobe by answering the following question: What five things do I need?

A PALETTE OF ONE

For those in search of the ultimate statement: Go monochrome. Find one color that represents you, and banish all others, cold turkey, from the closet. Black is a common choice. Many fair-haired women choose pale neutrals. Gloria Allred went with her namesake red.

Choosing a monochrome look is the closest female equivalent to the male uniform. And the result is a sophisticated, high-impact look that is unmistakably yours. And there's a surprise benefit, which black-suited businessmen discovered decades ago: Getting dressed, and shopping, become virtually stress- and decision-free.

SHAKE, RATTLE, AND ROLL

The rule against noisy jewelry eases as a signature style develops. You could be making a statement as your bracelet rattles against the conference table or jingles and clanks as you walk down the hall. However, remember the fable of the poor cat and the bell that the mice put around its neck.

3. Get Better Job

The Power of Positive Shopping
—Shop Smart

THE 80/20 RULE

It's a standard business statistic: 20% of your customers create 80% of the business. And the same ratio often applies to productivity in the workplace. But did you ever think that the same might be true of your closet? Pay attention to what you wear. Make note of it for a couple of weeks and you'll find that the colors, cuts and styles you wear are consistent. The fact is, most people wear 20% of their wardrobe 80% of the time. Buy carefully, know what you like, and you'll wear your entire wardrobe.

TAKE YOUR TIME—YOU'RE MAKING INVESTMENT CHOICES

The higher your rung on the corporate ladder, the greater the importance—and cost—of your clothes. Take your time when shopping to make sure you buy wisely. Only buy clothes that feel like a million bucks when you put them on—and that make you smile. At this point, you know what you like to wear (pantsuits, all beige, and bold earrings) and what you don't (dresses, bright colors, and flat shoes). Stick with what you like, but upgrade the quality. And by all means, hire the services of a personal shopper.

MARKET RESEARCH

At work, you run the show, and you've created teams of talented professionals to help you do it well. Now it's time to select a good closet crew to help keep your clothes current and in tip-top condition. The expert who is most indispensable to the working woman is the personal shopper. Whether hired privately or through a department store (where they are free of charge), the personal shopper can act as a market researcher for your closet, reporting what is new and appropriate for your needs, style, and status. He or she can teach you how to recognize quality, how to mix elements together, how to make a strong statement, even what looks are most compatible with your body and coloring. The best shoppers can direct you to the right hair and makeup expert. At your convenience, he will put together complete outfits for you to try

INVESTMENT DRESSING
The designer suit that was out of your price range in the early stages of your career may still be a stretch. But at this point, the splurge could be worth it: A finely tailored, well-designed suit is a long-term investment that can have a priceless return. The classic cut means you can wear it for years, and the extra quality and attention to detail translate into instant confidence, every time you put it on. This Giorgio Armani suit was photographed in 1995 for *Chic Simple Women's Wardrobe*, and still retains its style.

on, in a private dressing room or, sometimes, at your office or home. Most important, the personal shopper provides you with information and the goods you need while saving you precious time.

STYLE RESOURCES

Remember these names—they will be valuable resources as you upgrade your wardrobe:

Dry cleaner: All dry cleaners are not created equal. A good one can turn an item around for you in a day, expertly remove stains from delicate fabrics, and clean immaculately but gently and without the dreaded "dry cleaner scent." Word of mouth is the best reference. Treating surfaces like leather and suede might require a trip to a specialty cleaner—it's less convenient but worth the effort.

Tailor: A tailor you trust implicitly is crucial. Valuable traits to look for: Utter expertise in what is possible and what is not. Invisible handiwork. Thoroughness—someone who, when hemming pants, measures both the front and the back; when altering a skirt, measures from the floor up (the only way to form a straight hem); someone who teaches you something about clothes. Experience, experience, experience. Word of mouth is the best reference.

Shoe repairman: A mandatory member of your closet entourage if you want to keep all leather goods in shipshape condition. What has he done for you lately? Repaired your heel nicks and toe scuffs, kept your shoe surfaces smooth and polished and their soles sturdy; added holes to a belt and refreshed the sheen on your leather handbags. A shoe repairman even offers preventive measures, such as weatherproofing, toe taps, and protective soles. Visit him before the shoe is humiliatingly dilapidated—and often.

CHIC SIMPLE—PRACTICE, PRACTICE, PRACTICE

Like most things in life, dressing well takes practice. And the practice is a lifelong journey. With luck, the process becomes more refined—always a challenge yet increasingly gratifying. And as with other life endeavors, dressing to suit your identity should evolve as you do.

ASSESS. You know the drill by now. Assess—and try on—every item in your closet. Your goals and stature have changed. Have your clothes? Is your brand message clear?

DEJUNK. Be ruthless. Anything that is not communicating as

"Everyone thinks of changing the world, but no one thinks of changing himself."

LEO TOLSTOY

clearly and brilliantly as you are on the job, give away. This may mean parting with some perfectly good suits. Rest assured; they will be a godsend to someone just starting out and on a tighter budget. Consider donating to a charitable organization for a tax credit or a consignment shop to see a return on your investment.

RENEW. Now, what's missing? Gradually continue building your high-powered wardrobe. Develop your knowledge of and eye for exceptional quality. Work with a personal shopper. You are likely to buy more clothes now than ever before. Make sure they are statement makers, but that the statement never speaks louder than you do. Just because you can afford designer logos doesn't mean they're right for you. Are they compatible with your professional message? And just because you can buy the very best suits doesn't absolve you from needing the services of the very best tailor.

CLOTHES NO LONGER TALK, THEY COMMAND

A CEO dressed up as a slacker doesn't cut it anymore. A woman in a position of authority must project an equal amount of distinction in her dress and accessories. The cornerstone of the power wardrobe is still the suit, but at this stage of the game, it packs an extra punch.

shop smart

Power clothes make a loud and clear statement. Therefore purchasing them requires a little soul searching. Will you settle on the reliability of a logo? Search high and low to find items that uniquely represent you? Stick with the silhouettes, colors, and styles you have cultivated all along and simply upgrade their quality? This chapter gets to the nitty-gritty of the power purchase, whether it's a Grade A handbag, a wow-'em watch, or a suit that says "CEO" before you even open your mouth.

How to Buy a Power Outfit

SHOP SMART: STATEMENT SUIT

This suit gives an instant impression of authority—high-quality fabric, a strong silhouette, impeccable tailoring, and a perfect fit—and is often the result of a reasonable expenditure of money.

Why It Matters: Those in a position of authority must exude a similar level of distinction in their dress and accessories. To higher-ups, the suit conveys responsibility. To those beneath, it communicates a sense of command. A wardrobe of well-chosen power suits conveys consistency and personal style—and means you never again have to think about what you put on in the morning.

Quantity Counts: Composed of highly designed, coordinated pieces, a power suit makes a statement. And a statement is remembered. Therefore owning just one or two is not sufficient. At this stage of the game, you need—and can afford—more.

Getting Personalized: Every suit silhouette makes a statement. Try on many styles until you settle on one that suits your body type and reflects the image you want to convey.

SHOP SMART: BAGS AND SHOES

BAGS

The goal now is to downsize your hand-bags to reflect an upgrade in status. Choose small, streamlined bags—whether a clutch, folio, or attaché—that present an organized, no nonsense, unencumbered appearance. When achieving this level of success:

- Trade your tote for a slim leather portfolio.
- Replace your midsized handbag with a small structured bag (conveys order, authority, no nonsense).
- As ever, quality counts.
- Choose a smooth leather or more luxurious skins such as alligator, crocodile, or snake. Top grain leather bags are more durable than those made from split leather.
- A substantial lining aids longevity; leather is the best kind.
- Straps should be short and double-sided and piped or bound.

SHOES

Expanding a shoe wardrobe beyond the staple loafers and pumps is a sign of stature and success and can help bring color and personality to the pomp and circumstance of power clothes.

Power Wardrobe

Now it's time to fine-tune your wardrobe with clothes and accessories of exceptional quality and unmistakable style. The goal: A closetful of statement-making clothes that communicate success. This chapter will arm you with the resources to recognize and choose the right power suit for you; to develop a power palette; to cultivate a collection of accessories that convey personal and professional style; and to dress, when the situation demands, casually but with authority.

"The power to define the situation is the ultimate power."

JERRY RUBIN
Growing Up at Thirty-Seven

I'M IN CHARGE, DO I LOOK IT?

Double-Breasted

The most formal of suits, the double-breasted version has sharp lines, peaked lapels, and a disciplined, buttoned-up feel that add up to create an impression of powerful authority. Fabric is key; at this stage, a suit is only as good as its fabric. Look for a light, almost silky wool that has a graceful drape and doesn't wrinkle easily.

Competence, polish. A straight skirt to the knee, slightly nipped-in waist, well-shaped shoulders, and an impeccable fit (get thee to a tailor!). For ultimate conviction, pair with a crisp white shirt. Make sure the collar lies flat on the suit lapels. Keep buttoned up except for either top or bottom button.

DOUBLE-BREASTED = WORKPLACE WARRIOR.

Coatdress

I am woman, proclaims a coatdress, and I mean business. And there is no mistaking the seriousness of that business when the fabric is worked in a menswear pattern: Pinstripes, chalk stripes, glen plaids, mini houndstooth are all boardroom contenders.

Sophisticated authority. A menswear pattern with a notched collar equals can play with the boys and still be a woman. For a more relaxed alternative consider pairing with a black turtleneck, knee-high boots, and opaque tights in fall or winter. If belted, consider replacing the companion belt with one of higher caliber.

COATDRESS = FIERCELY FEMININE.

Long Jacket

A jacket that ventures beyond the norm (in other words, past hip level to somewhere between midcalf and the knee) says you are going to do it your way. This self-assured silhouette only works when the jacket is fitted (anything loose will look frumpy); and it must be worn only with its matching companion piece, whether it's a skirt, dress, or pants.

Elegant authority. A single-breasted jacket, pocket flaps that lie flat, paired with a shirt in a similar hue, a scoop-neck cashmere sweater, or nothing but a set of pearls.

LONG JACKET = CREATIVE, DRAMATIC.

Knit

A knit suit has good breeding. Coco Chanel liberated women by creating this uniform of comfort and feminine chic when she first introduced it during World War I. While its jacket and skirt—never pants—is softer and more feminine than the masculine inspired lines of a traditional suit, don't underestimate its power. The knit suit has been a favorite of former first ladies Nancy Reagan and Barbara Bush.

Quick but quaint (aka slightly old-school). A jacket cropped to the hip with a stand-up collar and placket-covered zipper. Pair with black patent leather pumps (for a high-polish edge) or neutral sling backs (for more discreet dignity). Because of texture and detailing, the components of a knit suit are effective only when worn together. For women who claim color as their mark of style, especially pastels, a knit suit is often preferred.

KNIT = REFINED AND SELF-ASSURED.

Color is

RED = Confidence, leadership, independence. Useful for presentations; shows security in one's role. Attracts attention.

Color is a quick means of communicating authority and style. A power color has added assets: It commands attention, conveys control, and, when properly chosen, sends a consistent message about your workplace identity.

POWERFUL.

ALL BLACK = Serious, sophisticated, determined— powerful and practical in urban environments.

Own a color. Pick a shade you like and make it your own. Wear it consistently. Choose one or two other colors that complement your personal uniform. A monochromatic look—a suit and shirt of matching colors—has high impact and is also elongating.

Pattern

Patterns pilfered from menswear can pack masculine punch, while adding texture and diversity to your wardrobe. Balancing bold pattern with a simple tailored silhouette and feminine detail is key.

HOUNDSTOOTH = UNAPOLOGETICALLY BOLD.

It used to be a
man's world…
now it's a
business world.

**PINSTRIPE =
POWER PLAYER;
STRONG
BUT SEXY;
AT THE TOP
OF ONE'S
GAME.**

Jewelry

GOLD LINK BRACELET
Subtle but strong, classic. Proper fit prevents
clanking; keep other jewelry in compatible metals.

PEARL-AND-GOLD FAUX EARRINGS
Bold and well-bred. Make sure not overly large
or small; keep other jewelry in compatible metals
and proportion.

One piece makes a statement,
two pieces becomes a report,
three, a committee.

CUFF BRACELET
Unapologetic impact, in-your-face style, modern. Wear with simple clothes that don't compete for visual impact; must fit perfectly on the wrist. To scream creativity and individuality, wear one on each wrist.

Time Piece

At this point in your career, you don't want "a watch," you want "The Watch." An emblem of status and efficiency, the watch has assumed a prominent position in business as a sign of success. If you're not drawn to a particular style, go for an all-time classic like the Rolex Oyster watch or the Cartier Tank, two of the most recognizable and copicd watches in history. Whatever you choose, don't skimp. This telling detail is what separates the women from the ingenues.

Alligator band.

Roman numerals reinforce formality.

Gold bezel.

Amethyst crown.

THE CARTIER TANK
French-designed and evocative of privilege, the Tank watch was conceived by Louis Cartier at the turn of the century after the flamboyant Brazilian aviator Alberto Santos Dumont remarked that it was difficult to pull a watch from a waistcoat while manning the controls of a biplane. It has since become a power perennial of unequaled status and popularity.

Old & New

You may be a "suit," as the saying goes, but the way you distinguish that suit is up to you. This is where personal style kicks in and can make a winning difference. Consider the impact of a lapel pin, whether it's a family heirloom filled with treasured photos or a modern design so distinctive it creates a style you can claim as your own.

ART JEWELRY

Twists of gold-filled strands that embrace precious and semi-precious stones, designer Kazuko's handmade jewelry is considered to be healing, a conduit of peace and well-being. The distinctive pieces can be worn as spiritual transmitters (don't knock it; everything helps in corporate America) or expressions of personal style.

HEIRLOOM

Whether it's been in the family for generations or not, an heirloom piece implies that success and style are in the genes.

Belts

Hermès "H" buckle
signals instant status.

REVERSE STATUS
Literally. The classic Hermès
"H" belt with its fine leather,
saddle stitching, and logo
buckle sports creative color
variations, such as blue on
one side, yellow on the other,
providing two belts in one.

If you're a belt wearer, by this point you're stocked up on basics. Now, enhance your collection: Choose one with a special buckle or designer logo. Status belts—in soft suedes or animal skins—signal authority on a casual dress day. And if you're a jewelry buff, try a metal chain belt.

CHAIN LINK
One of Paris designer Coco Chanel's fashion standards (along with multistrand pearls, quilted handbags, and two-tone sling backs) was the gold link belt, which epitomized her style philosophy: To make simplicity appear remarkable.

Scarf

A silk scarf gives a power suit, a silk blouse, or a cashmere sweater a mark of individuality and success. A designer label adds to the allure.

POWER HERITAGE

A perennial symbol of style, integrity, and substance, the Hermès scarf was first produced by the French luxury saddlery firm in 1937. Ever since, its 36-inch squares with equestrian and nature themes—whose hand-rolled borders and plush silk texture are trade secrets—have become a much-copied, but never-equaled, emblem of elegance.

Folio, Pen, and

The mantra for the promotion-minded: Speak softly and carry a small handbag. The smaller the bag, the more important the person. A tiny purse relays utter organization, effortlessness, and sense of control. Translation: Power.

PEN
Your writing piece should reflect the importance of your words. Don't be random about your choice in pens.

FOLIO
From boardroom to podium, a slim folio in exquisite leather and minimal detail to hold the bare essentials—speech, notepad, pen—says "On duty and in charge."

Clutch

CLUTCH

The smaller the bag, the bigger the success. Elegant
and refined, a clutch's petite, ladylike proportions
belies the power that it holds. At this stage, you
should have an expertly developed support system,
which leaves you unencumbered and able to navigate the heady ranks of business with ease.

STYLIZED
SPECTATORS
Feminine with flair.

ANKLE-STRAP
STILETTOS
Feminine,
fashionable.

PATENT LEATHER
MOCCASINS
Easygoing
prestige.

Shoe Wardrobe

Shoes bring personality to the pomp and circumstance of power clothes. They also reveal intention.
Are you daring or elegant? Are you going to kick
start the day or kick back? Well-designed shoes
inspire their wearer to stand tall and exude
confidence and authority.

BROWN SUEDE PUMP
Urban sophistication.

**CROCODILE
SLING BACKS**
Delicate but daring.

**SILK FAILLE
EVENING
PUMPS**
Instant
elegance.

Public Speaking

Success brings stardom. Or at least a greater call to step in front of an audience. Whether you're speaking at a marketing meeting, a client presentation, or an interview on television, every detail makes a heightened statement, and extra attention must be paid to send a clear, concise message. Consider who you are speaking to and the level of formality you need to project. How do you want the audience to relate to you? As a powerful leader? As accessible and one of them?

COLOR: On TV, avoid black, white, some reds (they tend to vibrate), and stripes (which "moiré" or squirm like an eel on camera). In general, choose a solid color that is attractive and inviting but not flamboyant. Blue, for example, has charisma.

SHAPE: In general, silhouettes should be simple and classic. Nothing should detract from what you are saying. For television, choose a structured jacket that will give your body shape.

ACCESSORIES: Minimal. Discreet accents are appropriate—a scarf, simple jewelry—but avoid anything overly eye-catching, reflective, or jangly.

HAIR: Should be brushed or pulled back from face to avoid temptation to fiddle.

READY FOR YOUR CLOSE-UP: Before stepping in front of the audience, do a last-minute appearance check. Make sure clothes are neat and in order. Check clothes, face, and teeth for renegade food morsels. Have a breath mint. Take a deep breath.

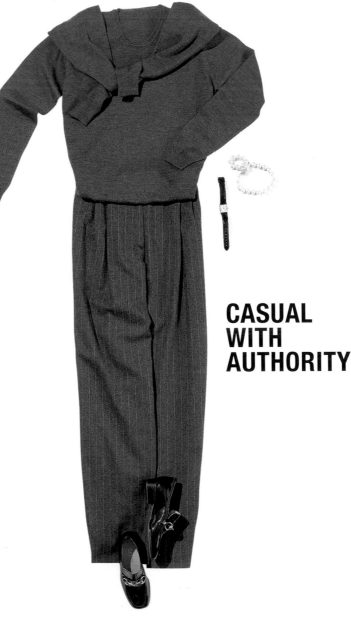

CASUAL WITH AUTHORITY

FORMAL
BUT
FRIENDLY

Powder bare
chest, neck,
and face to
reduce "shine."

Color is
eye-catching.
Pastels are
warm and
friendly.

The Power of Separates

UNIFYING LESSONS

BLUE-CHIP BLACK
A black backdrop easily pulls together separates while enhancing more colorful elements.

FINE KNIT
Power turtleneck is cashmere, not wool.

STRONG TAILORING
Textured wool blazer with dressmaker details.

STANDOUT HANDBAG
A graceful carryall.

CLASSIC PANTS
Well-designed trousers.

POWER DETAIL: COVERED BUTTONS

HOSIERY
Knee-highs should be opaque black so line is not broken between pant and shoe.

For many women, dressing casually (aka minus the suit) means a constant struggle to maintain an appearance of authority. The solution: Don't relax your standards. Wear a few power pieces—a blazer, a designer belt, killer shoes—with laid-back items that are of the utmost quality (a glen plaid skirt or a cashmere turtleneck).

BLACK SIMPLIFIES

POWER JACKET
Knit jacket with elegant gold buttons.

STANDOUT HANDBAG
High-quality tote
(in head-turning red).

DISTINCTIVE SKIRT
Glen plaid.

POWER DETAIL: PATTERN

HOSIERY
Should be opaque or semisheer black to keep
leg line long between skirt and boot.

The Power of Detail

LESSONS IN DETAIL

STATUS SHIRT
Distinctive details give the simple white shirt and skirt an authoritative edge.

FINE FABRIC
Fabric upgrade to high-quality cotton.

DOWN-TO-BUSINESS ACCESSORY
Cuff links.

SLEEK SHOES
Ultra-feminine heels.

POWER BAG
Choose a polished leather for a status look.

POWER DETAIL: FRENCH CUFF

HOSIERY
Black opaque is relaxed. Black semisheer dressier. Black sheer dressiest. Nude is freshest, looking almost bare-legged.

Whether it's a designer scarf, a cashmere sweater, or in-your-face feminine shoes, at this stage of the game, exquisite accents make the outfit.

DELUXE DETAILS

Elegant accessories and textures give sweater-dressing a dose of distinction.

FEMININE EXTRA
Striking silk scarf.

SLEEK SHOES
Designer pumps with dainty heel.

POWER BELT
Classic alligator.

FABRIC
Cashmere sweater with fashionable cowl.

COMPARTMENTALIZE
A quality leather and nylon tote can be practical and stylish.

POWER DETAIL: ALLIGATOR BELT

HOSIERY
Pants teamed with a pump with a dainty heel require a silky sheer or semisheer knee-high. But because the pump is so feminine, you can also wear a nude sock. Otherwise match socks to shoe or pant. If you choose a loafer you can go for a slightly heavier weight sock.

Wearing Leather

LEATHER LESSONS

SLEEK SUEDE
A single piece made of skin—a leather skirt, a suede jacket—gives well-chosen pieces instant sophistication.

FINE KNIT
Cashmere turtleneck.

POWER JACKET
Tailored suede jacket.

CLASSIC PANTS
Menswear-patterned pants.

SLEEK SHOES
Mile-high heels (for a dose of dressiness).

POWER DETAIL: SUEDE

HOSIERY
Knee-highs should be silky opaque or semisheer matching shoc and pant to keep line long and lean.

The key to wearing leather well:
Combine a single item with pieces that are low-key, high quality, and classic.

OFFICE LEATHER

FINE KNIT
A sporty sweater set in luxury cashmere.

DISTINCTIVE SKIRT
Leather pencil.

SLEEK SHOES
Sleek stiletto.

POWER DETAIL: LEATHER

HOSIERY
Should be opaque or semisheer to keep this look casual but very pulled together.

CLOSET power wardrobe

At this stage of your career (and life), you know who you are and your clothes represent your identity. Your suits have stature. Your shoes add a personal expression of yourself. Your handbags show organization and respectability. But does your closet represent that same level of fine-tuning and discernment? This may be a time when you want to bring in the closet professionals who can create the most efficient luxury closet, designed to all your wardrobe and aesthetic needs. But before you call, go through the Chic Simple Process to be sure you are sharing valuable real estate with clothes that count:

Assess—What do you own that lacks quality, is inappropriate, or dated for this level of success? Try on what's left. Does it fit well and feel comfortable?

DeJunk—Give away anything that doesn't support your developing identity and professional goals. If the clothes are of good quality, consider taking them to a consignment shop or donate them for a tax credit.

ReNew—What's missing? A jewelry box for your new collection of lapel pins? A pill remover to keep cashmere sweaters in tip-top shape? A way to organize your growing army of shoes? (Tip: keep the boxes stacked on shelves with a Polaroid of the shoes on the outside.)

CLOTHES CHECK

Group all evening clothes and accessories together. It's easier to assess what you have and what you need.

BLUE SKY BLUES

Dear Kim and jeff,
I'd like suggestions on what to wear while traveling—specifically for the twenty-some hours spent in planes and airports while traveling from the East Coast to Asia.
—Jetlagged

Dear Jetlagged,
You want a neat pulled-together appearance no matter where you are headed. When traveling, wear clothing that allows you to wiggle around in your seat while keeping you warm or cool depending on all the microclimates experienced en route. Dress in layers—like a knit sweater set—or carry a big wrap that can double as a blanket. Avoid fabrics that wrinkle easily and look for those with some stretch for added comfort. Wear pants and shoes that you can slip off when sleeping (and some cozy socks). And carry a zippered tote to hold your book and water. Travel gear is not only essential, but if attractive, can pull your entire look together.

—Kim and jeff

Goes with the Job

4

Travel and Entertainment Wardrobe

It's a reality of work life that's summed up by the pile of receipts crammed in your wallet. Traveling for business and entertaining clients are two very different endeavors, but they utilize the same set of skills: The ability to choose uncomplicated clothes that are appropriate to the location/occasion. This chapter addresses the possible pitfalls of, and smart solutions to, off-campus dressing.

4. Goes with the Job

Travel...
—All Dressed Up and Everywhere to Go

"You can't leave the haphazard to chance."

N. F. SIMPSON

DRESSING FOR TRAVEL

Packing for a business trip tends to induce fear: Of unknown circumstances, unfamiliar company, even unexpected weather patterns. All needless worries. Whether you're at a marketing meeting in Aruba or a client conference in Chicago, the goal is to bring clothes that represent your own identity and stature and that of your company. By following a few basic wardrobe principles, and using a little discipline, packing for business travel can give you a fresh outlook on your entire closet, and give you a crash course in a skill that will come in handy any time you take your wardrobe on the road: The clothes edit.

WHAT TO TAKE

The goal is to be prepared for every situation on your agenda—as well as any unexpected zingers that might pop up—with clothes that will send an upbeat, professional image of you and your company.

First, get an overview of your trip. Assess where you are going, for how long, and the purpose of your trip.

Consider dress codes: What type of firm are you doing business with—high-polish corporate or laid-back business appropriate? What is the purpose of your trip—a sales conference at a resort (relaxed but polished) or consulting work (traditional business dress)? What activities will you engage in during the trip (everything from client dinners to working out)? What is the weather forecast (check www.weather.com)?

READY TO GO
Save time by having makeup bags and toiletry kits always packed on a "trip shelf."

Finally, call ahead to determine the particulars of the place you are staying: Does the hotel have a gym? Hair dryers? Offer laundry and dry-cleaning service?

The idea is to pack a few key pieces that can be worn in a variety of ways. For example: 1 suit + 1 sweater set + 1 black dress + 1 pair of black pants = 11 outfits that can fit into one bag.

Unless you're traveling to extreme climates, seasonless fabrics that don't wrinkle easily serve best: Tropical wool, lightweight wool with stretch, techno stretch, cotton for tops, silk, featherweight cashmere, lightweight merino wool knit, jersey, wool crepe (dressy). A coat made of microfiber is lightweight and will brave most weather conditions.

While you're packing, lay everything on the bed, which will help you visualize what you're bringing and what you're missing. For maximum versatility, choose a neutral-colored suit and make sure each additional item you pack goes with it. What you wear on top is more memorable than on the bottom, so bring accessories (a pretty scarf) and splashes of color (a bright blouse) that will change the look of a skirt and/or pair of pants. Stick with simple shapes and minimal patterns. Before packing, try on each outfit. Make sure you have underwear that works with everything you're bringing (do you need a strapless bra? did you bring heels high enough for the hem on your pants?).

regional guidelines

General Guidelines: Geography isn't as important as it once was in determining how we dress. As the world population is exposed to more and more of the same influences, tastes, inevitably, have become more global, less local. So when traveling for business, basic professional attire is appropriate just about anywhere in the world. Still, to understand regional subtleties—and to avoid looking like a tourist—it is helpful to understand the tendencies in different parts of the United States and the world. You should be able to remix items from your existing wardrobe to suit any destination.

Dress Smart Wherever You Go

MIDWEST (CHICAGO AND DETROIT)

Cities like Chicago and Detroit are more cosmopolitan than other parts of the Midwest, and women dress up for work in suits. In Minneapolis and other regional cities, women are comfortable with a more workday, casual look, wearing khakis and sweater sets.

Evening: A lot of entertaining is corporate in the Midwest. Black-tie fund-raising events take place quite often in these cities, especially on weekends. Women wear cocktail dresses or pantsuits to black-tie events in dressy fabrics like velvet and satin. Accessories are dressy and unique. Velvet scarves, cashmere shawls, and beaded evening bags are popular. Preferred colors for formal dress in the Midwest are black, deep browns, midnight navies, and dark purples.

NORTHEAST (BOSTON)

Boston is an intellectual city, which gives rise to individualism and trend-setting. However, there is a division between suburban and urban women in terms of fashion. The suburban woman is slightly more conservative and wears brighter colors and lower hemlines. The city woman prefers trendier fashions in more subdued colors and with higher hemlines.

Evening: Urban and suburban women prefer the little black evening dress but personalize it with a jacket. Because of the cobblestone streets and the periodically inclement weather, women most often wear low heels.

NORTHEAST (NEW YORK)

New York City is considered the fashion hub of the country, and businesswomen are fashion-conscious and impeccably groomed, yet iconoclastic. Colors are urban standard: black, charcoal, chocolate, beige, white, and splashes of color. Pedicures, manicures, a well-maintained hairstyle and color, and groomed eyebrows are essentials. Well-tailored suits are standard in most industries. However, the city's many creative fields—music, publishing, film, fashion—allow for an individual's personal style in the workplace.

Evening: For most formal parties, long dresses with quality accessories will do nicely; the old-money society set dresses simply and elegantly for black-tie charity functions; for glitterati-literati openings and events, women dress dramatically, and not necessarily in a traditionally formal manner. The newest, cutting-edge designs are popular. Many New York women own a little black dress, which can be worn to a variety of events simply by adding or subtracting accessories. Many people are label-conscious. They often mix separates, which contributes to enormous personal style, a hallmark of New York dressing. Suburban New Yorkers are much more relaxed and colorful.

NORTHEAST
(WASHINGTON, DC)

The suit is key in DC and traditionally a realm where women can shine and pull focus through color, though more and more are being lured by a uniform of basic black. The quilted Chanel-like bag is popular and the no-nonsense suit is worn after dark, dressed up with a scarf or pin. A lot of women buy clothing through catalogs. Women in DC tend to avoid making overt fashion statements and generally frown upon seductive dressing, preferring that their political views, power, and influence make their statement.

Evening: Entertaining in Washington often takes place in the home. Politics is the talk—read the newspapers, magazines, and listen to the news on TV and radio to keep up. Mixing Democrats and Republicans can liven things up. People's political standings may change, but as Sally Quinn, a Washington journalist and hostess, says, "You should never count anyone out in Washington, because they always come back."

PACIFIC NORTHWEST
(SEATTLE)

Women are more concerned with being comfortable than with being on the cutting edge of fashion. Precious high heels and suede shoes don't last long in a city where it rains frequently. Many women wear sneakers on the street to preserve their dress shoes. Working women tend to dress business casual, wearing pants, blouses, and sweaters and only resorting to suits for the occasional crucial meeting. Soft leather shoulder bags are popular. Structured handbags are considered overly formal. Accessories are where women indulge in being fashionable: This season's choker or branded belt buckle may be the way a woman updates her look.

Evening: For formal occasions, women tend to wear a classic dress (hem to the knee; not a cocktail suit) in black or jewel tones.

THE ROCKIES (DENVER)

Dressing for work in the Rockies is business casual: Pants or khakis with a blouse, sweater, or crisp white shirt. In the eighties, many Texans moved to the area, imparting some of their characteristic fashion flashiness to the social scene. In other words, color and accessories like belts and earrings are key.

Evening: There are more charity functions per capita in Denver than in any other city in the country, providing many occasions for formal dress. Women's evening wear is understated and elegant. The little black cocktail dress predominates, but women will wear ankle-length gowns for very grand events. Many events in Denver call for "creative Western elegance." Women typically wear broomstick skirts and matching Western jackets with nickel or silver conch buttons.

SOUTHEAST (ATLANTA)

All in all, Atlanta is a casual city, but the city's booming business sector has attracted people from around the world, and the professional dress code is fast becoming that of a larger metropolis.

Women wear conservative suits or business appropriate skirts or pants and blouses, with midheight heels. Black is not a popular choice in this vibrant city. On the contrary, teal, gold, red, and pastels are prevalent colors among women. Traditional taboos are respected: After Memorial Day and before Labor Day is the only period of the year to wear black patent leather shoes or white shoes. No matter how hot temperatures may stay after summer, women dress strictly for the season.

Some of the strict Southern fashion rules seem to be fading in Atlanta. Society women wear khakis, the "great white shirt," and expensive loafers, belts, and bags when they shop and lunch.

Evening: Women are practical but not prissy. Style is always ladylike, which is the most important dressing guideline for women. Tailored feminine elegance is admired more than trendy extremes; women prefer clothing that can be worn both to the office and to the symphony.

SOUTHWEST (HOUSTON)

Texas women have a well-deserved reputation for being the most dressed, if not the best dressed, in the nation. Career women wear skirt or pantsuits in bright colors with feminine blouses. It is not unusual for women in Houston or Dallas to change clothes three times a day (exercise clothes, business attire, evening wear). Heat, humidity, bitter cold, and the chill of air-conditioning have a lot to do with this. "To Bare or Not to Bare" is one of the biggest controversies in the South and Southwest, but women here, in spite of the heat and discomfort, continue to wear stockings—usually panty hose—for business, weddings, church, luncheons, and most evening events. The only time women here may remove their stockings is when they are wearing extremely casual clothes with flat shoes or if they are "fashion forward."

Evening: Unlike in many other cities, career women almost always change clothes for the evening, whether it's a cocktail suit, dress, or formal wear. If a woman has good jewelry—stones one might refer to as "jewels" rather than jewelry—she wants clothes that show these off.

TROPICAL (MIAMI)

Business wear has been influenced by the influx of South and Central Americans conducting business in this region. Clothing is more feminine than in other cities, with shorter hemlines and higher heels. Business attire has a light, tropical feel, with suits tending toward light neutrals and dresses more prevalent than they are in other cities.

TROPICAL (PALM BEACH)

Though they're geographically close, Miami and Palm Beach are worlds apart. Palm Beach sports an old-school, old-money look. Business attire in the two cities is similar.

WEST COAST (LOS ANGELES)

Business dressing is divided into three categories in Los Angeles, and all of them revolve around, or take their cues from, Hollywood: 1. The execs—the people who work in the offices and make decisions about money—wear dark suits, whether they're men or women. LA is less designer label-conscious than a city like New York. 2. The creatives execs—agents, PR executives, and producers all fall into this category—dress corporate creative, which means trendy, hip clothes that have professional polish: Form-fitting pants with a crisp white shirt or T-shirt and a suede jacket; a skirt or dress with boots. 3. The talent—anyone from an actress to a director—dress extremely casual, while still being responsive to the season's new trends.

Evening: Aside from red carpet events, LA occasions rarely call for formal attire. Gallery openings, book parties, ballets, the theater, and the symphony do not require dressing up. One might wear pants and a top, possibly a jacket, to most of them, unless it were an opening night, and then a pantsuit in silk or linen. At a museum party or slightly formal affair, a cocktail dress will be worn, and more pantsuits in silk or linen. At movie premieres, the stars wear short dresses or pantsuits, always designer wear, sometimes mixed with vintage clothes. Everyone else comes from work and is very casual because the movies all start at 7:30.

WEST COAST (SAN FRANCISCO)

Women are sophisticated, formal, and European in style. Weather is variable (long springs, cool summers; September and October are the warmest months) and demands a seasonless wardrobe. Light wool crepes and seasonless silks are favored; there is little need for heavy winter overcoats or clothing for steamy climates. Women here enjoy forward-looking style. Day-to-evening looks are popular because so many people go to an early dinner straight from work. Sweater sets work well because the temperature drops at night. People look pulled together and would rather overdress than dress too casually.

international guidelines

As technology has made the wide world smaller and smaller, Western business attire has become appropriate just about anywhere on the planet. Nonetheless, an awareness of regional customs and attitudes is critical and will help you to show the proper decorum and respect in every situation you encounter, whether it's favoring pantsuits and scant makeup when in China, or shunning overly androgynous looks when conducting business in Russia.

Dress Smart All Over the World

IN GENERAL:

- Most countries—especially developing countries—are more conservative in dress than the U.S. Skirts are longer, blouses tend not to be low-cut, clothing is not worn tight. Consult a guidebook to learn the specific customs of the place you are visiting. You will feel more comfortable, and so will your hosts.
- Style in cities is often less conservative than it is in rural areas.
- Be prepared for very specific rules regarding dress whenever you are visiting a religious site. The usual code involves covering your head, arms, legs, and feet—or some combination thereof. Slip-on shoes can be very useful for visiting shrines and mosques, as you will be expected to wear slippers or socks inside. A scarf can be an instant hat, convenient for respecting local customs.
- Steer clear of native dress unless you learn otherwise. It can look patronizing and silly.
- Bring at least one bathing suit that has some coverage, until you're sure about how much skin is too much on the beach.
- Bring something nice for the evening. It doesn't have to be fancy, but in most places outside the U.S. people change clothes for dinner. In some countries you may be eating on a floor or mat; it's important that you dress appropriately and comfortably so that you will be able to bend your legs to the side without being too revealing.

AFRICA

Dressing neatly and cleanly is a sign of respect. It is important to wear well-pressed clothing, particularly when visiting a private home or a business office. Dress codes tend to be more formal in English-speaking countries, less so in French-speaking countries. In rural areas, skirts should generally be below the knee. Arms and shoulders should be covered at all times. Formal wear is rarely required. Avoid dressing in safari clothes for business; it can be seen as an offensive reminder of colonialism. It is crucial not to wear camouflage or military dress. In some countries this dress may be perceived as that of a mercenary, while in others it is actually illegal.

Throughout the Ivory Coast, residents dress primarily in the French style and are very fashion-conscious. Loose pants and dresses are both stylish and comfortable. In Zimbabwe, dress is quite Westernized. Loose-fitting pants or skirts that are not revealing are appropriate.

In Uganda, unlike in many other African countries, it is appreciated when Westerners wear the national dress on special occasions. This long cotton gown with a sash is called a busuti. At other times, a dress or skirt is appropriate, especially in villages.

ASIA

Many Asian countries can be very hot and humid, so you will want to pack clothing made of natural, not synthetic, fibers. Because they breathe, fabrics made of natural fibers are much more comfortable. Cotton, linen, and silk are best. Also, hosiery may not be necessary in countries where it is extremely hot.

China: Pantsuits are particularly appropriate, since Chinese women often wear pants. It is customary in China to wear as little makeup and jewelry as possible. High heels, expensive purses, and flashy designer clothes are viewed as extravagant and unnecessary—except in Hong Kong; here, designer clothes and accessories are a status symbol, though the style and color tend to remain conservative.

Japan: Formal business wear is the rule, which for women means conservative dresses and sleek suits worn with heels. All neutral colors are appropriate, except black, which is viewed as funereal. Red is considered flashy and inappropriately sexy. Overcoats are considered unclean, so it is important to remove them in the hallway and carry them, rather than wearing them into an office. In private homes or restaurants, you may be seated on tatami mats during dinner. You will be expected to remove your shoes at the entrance. Wear good hosiery and a loose skirt, and sit with your knees bent and to one side.

The exchange of business cards is almost ceremonial. The proper way to exchange is presenting your card held in two hands with the print facing the recipient. When you are the recipient, receive the card with care and respect. Take a few moments to read the business card you have been given before tucking it carefully away. Do not write on a business card. It would be considered insulting. Also avoid direct eye contact.

For traveling outside Tokyo, comfortable shoes, slacks, sweaters, blouses, and jackets are appropriate for a pulled-together yet relaxed look.

Korea: Businesswomen dress modestly and wear suits with skirts or dresses— no pants. Sitting on the floor is customary, so skirts that are too tight or narrow should be avoided.

Philippines: Among the most dapper dressers in Asia, Filipinos expect formal business attire (skirts and dresses more than pants).

Malaysia: Yellow is the color of royalty and should not be worn to formal functions or when visiting the palace.

Pakistan: The native dress is welcomed.

It consists of a long blouse, called a kameez, worn over pants, called salwar. Jackets are excellent business wear because they look professional and are not too revealing.

Thailand: Businesswomen are sharp, fashion-conscious dressers with modest, conservative style. Black is considered funereal here, unless strongly accented with color. Don't show the bottom of your feet or the soles of your shoes. It is considered insulting.

Vietnam: Conservative dresses or professional blouses worn with pants are the norm.

EUROPE

Business dress throughout Europe is on par with dress codes in the United States.

England: The climate is a little cool and often rainy. Be prepared. The dress is conservative in general, although there is a lot of exciting cutting-edge fashion coming out of London.

France: French women are known for their quiet, discreet elegance. They know to buy less, but better quality.

Italy: Italians are very chic and enjoy wearing rich colors and textures. They consider all black too serene and mournful. Glamorous Italian women are bare-legged in the summer and usually wear gold jewelry.

ISRAEL

Business appropriate dressing has evolved here, and suits have become commonplace. Women often shun hosiery, however, when the heat and humidity rise.

MEXICO

Most business is conducted in cosmopolitan Mexico City, where women wear suits or dresses with high heels, makeup, and jewelry.

RUSSIA

Business attire in Russia runs the gamut from corporate to flamboyant. Businesswomen tend to dress in unabashedly feminine clothes, as androgynous styles are less understood and somewhat looked down upon. And it is not unusual for both genders to wear an outfit several days running. Since temperatures swing to extremes, dressing in layers is advisable.

SOUTH AMERICA

Corporate business attire is customary. Locals tend to dress more conservatively on the west coast than on the east.

SPAIN

Spaniards are a well-dressed, well-groomed group, wearing tailored suits of good design.

AUSTRALIA AND NEW ZEALAND

During the day, conservative work clothes are the norm. Keep in mind that the seasons are a mirror image of the North, so in December it's summer and in July it's midwinter. The women of Brisbane wear similar styles as the women of Houston or Dallas—casual and simple lightweight clothing, especially dresses, with gold jewelry and bright makeup. In summer months, women prefer lighter colors and navy. In Sydney, women are very aware of labels. They are among the most "fashion forward" of all Australians.

INTERNATIONAL SIZING

When traveling keep in mind that clothes and shoes are sized differently in other countries.

dresses, coats, suits, skirts, pants													
UNITED STATES	4	6	8	10	12	14	16	18					
GREAT BRITAIN	8	10	12	14	16	18	20	20					
EUROPE	32	34	36	38	40	42	44	48					
shoes													
UNITED STATES	4	4½	5	5½	6	6½	7	7½	8	8½	9	9½	10
GREAT BRITAIN	2½	3	3½	4	4½	5	5½	6	6½	7	7½	8	8½
EUROPE	35	35½	36	36½	37	37½	38	38½	39	39½	40	40½	41

Travel Wardrobe

Packing smart is like fashion math: It can make a handful of pieces add up to many different looks. When traveling, wardrobe principles work overtime and a tight edit is mandatory. The key: Loving every item you pack and making sure it's just right for the business at hand. In the end, learning your packing math will lead to the ultimate style solution: You'll look twice as good with half as much.

"Is there anything as horrible as starting on a trip? Once you're off, that's all right, but the last moments are earthquake and convulsion, and the feeling that you are a snail being pulled off your rock."

ANNE MORROW LINDBERGH
Hour of Gold, Hour of Lead

WHAT'S MY TRAVEL UNIFORM?

How to Pack

When traveling for business, your luggage must be: 1. As efficient as your filing system; 2. As presentable as your nicest suits; and 3. Practical enough to transport those suits (and blouses and shoes) to your final destination neatly and safely.

- Pieces should match. Solid colors are preferable. Keep in good condition.
- Don't take more pieces than you can haul through an airport without help.
- Bag should always have proper ID (include a business card) and a colorful tag to make it easy to spot.
- Place a copy of your itinerary in suitcase for easy contact in case it is lost.
- Carrying a duffel bag on a business trip is like wearing sweatpants to a board meeting.
- Fabric matters. Luggage should be sturdy. If choosing nylon, go with ballistic, which is one of the strongest at about 1,000 denier (a number system indicating width and strength of the fibers). For the average business traveler, about 420-denier nylon or 600-denier polyester should be adequate.

WHEELIE
Packing assets: A built-in garment bag, easy-maneuver wheels, and a retractable handle that is long enough to pull without strain.

OVERNIGHTER
Your carry-on should look as respectable as you do. Be sure it's not too heavy or otherwise awkward to carry.

GARMENT BAG
The idea behind garment bags is that your clothing hangs in the bag as it does in your closet. To avoid wrinkling, double bag each garment within dry-cleaning plastic.

HOW TO PACK

1. First interlock belts and run them along the inner circumference of your suitcase.
2. Next pack heavy or bulky items—shoes, toiletry kit (keep a toothbrush in your handbag).
3. Add a layer of tissue or plastic between garments—allows clothes to slide, not rub, preventing wrinkling.
4. To pack pants: Fold at the seam and drape lengthwise in suitcase, with legs hanging over one end. Add a layer of tissue or plastic, and leave hanging while you…
5. Add sweaters, shirts, then lighter items (shells, scarves), and another layer of tissue.
6. Fold pant legs back across suitcase.
7. Double bag hanging garments with plastic.
8. Bring a stuff sack for undies or other loose garments.

STUFF SACKS

The stuff sack is an innovation that revolutionized backpacking. In business travel, where packing is an art and utility a science, stuff sacks not only solve the problem of where things should go, but allow specific items to be located quickly and easily. When using stuff sacks, different color sacks can identify various contents—from hosiery to electronics. Mesh sacks are lightweight, see-through, and let water easily evaporate. A Ziploc bag also makes a great stuffer, especially for things that are wet like swimsuits or gym clothes.

What to Pack

- Start with a suit in a neutral color.
- Choose tops, handbags, shoes, and other accessories that go with that suit.
- Keep patterns to a minimum.
- Use accessories or accents of color to change a look (people remember what's on top more than the bottom).
- Lay everything out on your bed to help you visualize compatibility and recognize what's missing.
- Simple shapes go best with many things.
- Dress in layers to adjust to climate changes.
- Try everything on before packing.
- Make sure underwear works with your clothes.
- If traveling for more than three days, consider laundering your undergarments in your room.
- Love everything you pack.
- Carry your jewelry, medicine, cell phone, and any important information with you at all times.
- Pack garments that don't wrinkle easily.

CARRY-ON TOTE

COMPUTER CASE

AGENDA

PASSPORT HOLDER

CELL PHONE CASE

GARMENT BAG

ACCESSORIES CASE

SHOE BAG

...One Week

1. THE IDEA
2 suits
2–3 pairs of shoes
5 tops
1 dress
1 coat
tote
smaller bag
undergarments
optional: exercise clothes

2. THE REALITY
black suit
beige suit
3 pairs of shoes: black flats, evening shoes, lighter
   color sensible heel
red sheath dress
5 tops: black nylon tee, beige knit shell, white silk
   blouse, black turtleneck, light-blue sweater set

3. THE APPLICATION

DAY	A.M.	P.M.	EXTRAS
MONDAY - TRAVEL DAY	black suit w/ black tee	ditto	black flats, change to pumps for dinner
TUESDAY	meeting: beige suit w/ beige shell	cocktail dinner: red dress, pearls	day: beige pumps night: black pumps (hose)
WEDNESDAY	FREE DAY!: beige skirt & blue sweater, SWIM STUFF	dinner meeting: black pants & white silk blouse	black pumps, pearls, & little bag
THURSDAY	breakfast & lunch meeting: beige skirt, black suit jacket, turtleneck	room service!!!	beige pumps
FRIDAY	SWIM, shop!	dinner meeting: red dress, black suit jacket	black pumps, pearls, & little bag
SATURDAY	all day conference: black pants, sweater set	ditto	black flats
SUNDAY - TRAVEL DAY	black pants w/ black turtleneck	ditto	definitely black flats

The packing chart—the days you will be traveling go in a vertical column. Make three adjacent columns to designate what to wear in the A.M. and P.M. and a column for extras (exercise gear). Fill in what you plan to wear. Mix up clothing separates to avoid packing a lot.

Travel Clothes

No matter how stylish the outfit, if it doesn't travel well, it doesn't travel. Clothes worn in transit should be one part practical, and one part presentable. You are representing your company, even off duty.

SUIT
Essential for business in a fabric with stretch (for comfort) that doesn't wrinkle easily.

PANTS
Travel with ease.

SUNGLASSES
Don't leave home without them.

BAG
Good quality and a size to accommodate carry-on necessities.

FLAT SHOES
Comfortable navigating throughout airports and easy to slip off en route.

SMART OPTIONS:
- A lightweight microfiber coat.
- A pashmina wrap, which can double as a blanket.
- Cozy socks.

Travel Wardrobe

1 BAG   7 PIECES   11 OCCASIONS

1. gray suit with pink camisole = meeting
2. gray suit with blue knit top = presentation
3. gray pants with pink camisole = drinks with client
4. gray pants with sweater set = visit plant
5. gray pants with blue knit top = dinner with client
6. black pants with pink camisole = award dinner
7. black pants with blue knit top = night off
8. black pants with sweater set = seminar
9. black dress with cardigan = lunch meeting
10. black dress with gray suit jacket = breakfast meeting
11. black dress = cocktails

THE SUIT
The most versatile travel staple when worn together (for ultimate authority), or as individual pieces mixed with others, for infinite business looks.

THE SWEATER SET
Has a hint of suit-jacket decorum (but better suit-case-fitting skills) and can give a fresh dash of color and femininity to any pants, suit, or skirt.

BLACK PANTS
A go-with-everything base for a suit jacket, while shirt, beaded evening camisole, and more. Travels well: Doesn't show dirt or wrinkle easily.

BLACK DRESS
With different accessories—from a daytime jacket and scarf to bare-armed with pearls and stilettos—it completely transforms.

PACKING CHART—THE POWER OF A SPREADSHEET

One of the most efficient uses of spreadsheet software? Creating a detailed (okay, some say obsessive) packing list. As you learn what works and what you were missing, make a record of it, so that with each trip you become more efficient.

ITEM	MONDAY	TUESDAY	WEDNESDAY	THURSDAY	FRIDAY	ITEM
UNDERWEAR						**UNDERWEAR**
BRA						BRA
PANTIES						PANTIES
SLIP						SLIP
CONTROL TOP						CONTROL TOP
HOSIERY						**HOSIERY**
PANTY HOSE						PANTY HOSE
SOCKS						SOCKS
SUIT						**SUIT**
JACKET						JACKET
SKIRT						SKIRT
PANTS						PANTS
SEPARATES						**SEPARATES**
TOPS:						TOPS:
shirt/blouse						shirt/blouse
T-shirt						T-shirt
sweater						sweater
turtleneck						turtleneck
JACKET						JACKET
SKIRT						SKIRT
PANTS						PANTS
ACCESSORIES						**ACCESSORIES**
PURSE						PURSE
BAG						BAG
BELT						BELT
JEWELRY						JEWELRY
WATCH						WATCH
GLASSES						GLASSES
SUNGLASSES						SUNGLASSES
SHOES						**SHOES**
HEELS						HEELS
FLATS						FLATS
PUMPS						PUMPS
OUTERWEAR						**OUTERWEAR**
RAINCOAT						RAINCOAT
COAT						COAT
SCARF						SCARF
GLOVES						GLOVES
HAT						HAT
UMBRELLA						UMBRELLA
OTHER						**OTHER**
WORKOUT						WORKOUT
SWIMSUIT						SWIMSUIT
EVENING						EVENING
SPORT						SPORT

PACKING LISTS

REASONS FOR MAKING A PACKING LIST

1. To simplify and organize the packing process.
2. To control the number of items packed.
3. To prevent the omission of vital items.
4. To guard against over-packing.
5. To help clarify clothing options and combinations.
6. To assist with claims against lost luggage.

BUSINESS TRIP
- ❏ Address book
- ❏ Advertising materials
- ❏ Airline tickets
- ❏ Appointment book
- ❏ Briefcase
- ❏ Business cards
- ❏ Calculator
- ❏ Computer, accessories
- ❏ Confirmations—hotel, etc.
- ❏ Correspondence
- ❏ Credit cards
- ❏ Expense forms
- ❏ Files
- ❏ Highlighters
- ❏ Letters of credit
- ❏ Markers
- ❏ Meeting materials
- ❏ Money
- ❏ Notebooks
- ❏ Paper clips
- ❏ Passport
- ❏ Pencils/pens
- ❏ Portfolio
- ❏ Presentation materials
- ❏ Price lists
- ❏ Proposals
- ❏ Publications
- ❏ Purchase order forms
- ❏ Reports
- ❏ Rubber bands
- ❏ Samples
- ❏ Stamps
- ❏ Stapler, staples
- ❏ Stationery, envelopes
- ❏ Tape recorder, tapes
- ❏ Time records
- ❏ Work pads

OVERNIGHT
- ❏ Toiletry kit
- ❏ Nightclothes
- ❏ Shirt
- ❏ Socks, stockings
- ❏ Underwear

CARRY-ON
- ❏ Address book
- ❏ Camera, film
- ❏ Car/house keys
- ❏ Confirmations
- ❏ Electronic equipment
- ❏ Eyeglasses—regular, sun
- ❏ Foreign language dictionary
- ❏ Handbag
- ❏ Identification
- ❏ Jewelry
- ❏ Medicine
- ❏ Money
- ❏ Outerwear
- ❏ Passport, visas
- ❏ Portable CD player
- ❏ Reading material
- ❏ Ticket
- ❏ Toothbrush, toothpaste
- ❏ Water

BASIC CLOTHES
- ❏ Belt
- ❏ Black dress
- ❏ Black shoes
- ❏ Bodysuit, leggings
- ❏ Handbag
- ❏ Hosiery, underwear
- ❏ Jeans
- ❏ Jewelry
- ❏ Raincoat
- ❏ Scarf
- ❏ Shorts
- ❏ Sleepwear
- ❏ Sneakers
- ❏ Sports clothes
- ❏ Suit with pants and skirt
- ❏ Sweater
- ❏ Swimsuit, sarong
- ❏ T-shirt
- ❏ Vest
- ❏ Walking shoes
- ❏ Watch
- ❏ White shirt

TRAVEL KIT
- ❏ Baggies for spillables
- ❏ Bath oil
- ❏ Birth control
- ❏ Body lotion
- ❏ Cleanser
- ❏ Compact
- ❏ Cosmetic kit:
  - ❏ Blush
  - ❏ Concealer
  - ❏ Eye pencil
  - ❏ Eye shadow
  - ❏ Eyelash curler
  - ❏ Eyeliner
  - ❏ Face powder
  - ❏ Foundation
  - ❏ Lip balm
  - ❏ Lip liner
  - ❏ Lipstick
  - ❏ Mascara
  - ❏ Nail polish
- ❏ Cotton balls
- ❏ Cotton swabs
- ❏ Dental floss
- ❏ Dentures, case, cleaner
- ❏ Deodorant
- ❏ Douche bag/lotion
- ❏ Emery boards
- ❏ Eye cream
- ❏ Eye makeup remover
- ❏ Foot powder
- ❏ Hair care:
  - ❏ Bobby pins
  - ❏ Clips
  - ❏ Comb
  - ❏ Curlers
  - ❏ Curling iron
  - ❏ Dryer
  - ❏ Rubber bands
  - ❏ Scrunchies
  - ❏ Spray
- ❏ Hand lotion
- ❏ Makeup remover
- ❏ Moisturizer
- ❏ Mouthwash
- ❏ Nail polish remover pads
- ❏ Night cream
- ❏ Perfume
- ❏ Razor, blades
- ❏ Sanitary products
- ❏ Sewing kit
- ❏ Shampoo, conditioner
- ❏ Shower cap
- ❏ Soap, box
- ❏ Sunscreen
- ❏ Tissues
- ❏ Tweezers

MEDICINE CHECKLIST
- ❏ Antiseptic lotion
- ❏ Aspirin
- ❏ Band-Aids
- ❏ Cold remedies
- ❏ Diarrhea medication
- ❏ Emergency contacts
- ❏ Identification bracelet
- ❏ Insect repellent
- ❏ Medical information— allergies, medications, blood type
- ❏ Moleskin for blisters
- ❏ Physician's name, address, telephone
- ❏ Prescription medications
- ❏ Sunblock
- ❏ Thermometer
- ❏ Throat lozenges
- ❏ Vitamins

INTERNATIONAL CHECKLIST
- ❏ Addresses for correspondence
- ❏ Auto registration (if driving)
- ❏ Cash, including some in the currency of the country to which you are traveling
- ❏ Credit cards
- ❏ Emergency contacts
- ❏ Extra prescription glasses and contacts
- ❏ Insurance papers
- ❏ International driver's license
- ❏ Lightweight tote bag for purchases
- ❏ Medical information
- ❏ Passport, visas, health certificates
- ❏ Phrase book or dictionary
- ❏ Tickets and travel documents
- ❏ Travel itinerary
- ❏ Traveler's checks and personal checks

4. Goes with the Job

... & Entertainment
—Relax, It's Only Your Career

"No lady
is ever a
gentleman."

JAMES BRANCH CABELL

DRESS SMART WHEN YOU DRESS UP

If work only consisted of work—accomplishing the tasks at hand—this book wouldn't be necessary. But as we have discussed, work is also about appearances and impressions, confidence and perceptions. And nowhere is this hazy style requirement more complicated than in the social side of work, the dance of "entertaining." Whether you're taking clients to dinner, attending the Christmas party, or representing your company at a charity event, the entire playing field changes.

It's important to remember that such social events are a continuation of the art of business. Making informed decisions about your clothes, and the etiquette that goes with them, can be critical to advancing in or maintaining a career.

DANGER ZONES: DRESSING AT RELAXED OCCASIONS

When business wanders into a leisure setting, there are pitfalls where you least expect them: Instead of issues of skirt length, it's proper swimwear (one-piece only, covered up unless swimming) and the sheerness of your sarong (none). Instead of "jacket required?" it's "khakis crisp enough?" (or "are my khakis passable?") Here, a few words of wisdom regarding casual career moments.

CONVENTIONS

The standard dress at a convention: On duty but at ease. In other words, dress as you would on your most casual day at the office (casual Fridays excluded). Men tend to wear a jacket but no tie. For women, pants, a turtleneck, and a nice belt or pants and a blouse send the right message.

SALES CONFERENCES

At a sales conference, the dress code is business casual, which means a wardrobe of crisp, clean "play" clothes that have a polish of being brand new. The goal: To look laid-back and just professional enough.

RETREATS

It's that odd phenomenon that sends groups of coworkers fleeing to warmer climes in order to relax, sometimes strategize, and build camaraderie. In such settings, many individuals confuse dressed down with downright slack   which is not a place you want to go if you want to go anyplace. As with a sales conference, the solution is to look casual but polished.

LIGHTS, CAMERA...

Dressing up for business doesn't mean full hair and movie makeup. Excess is distracting, while no makeup looks unprofessional. Overall you should look like you do during your workday—neat and well-groomed—but you may want to perk things up a bit: Perhaps by getting a manicure or having your hair professionally styled or blown dry. Makeup can be subtly enhanced, but only play up either the eyes or the lips. If in doubt, go for a professional consultation. Most beauty counters at department stores offer this service for free. And go easy on the fragrance.

shop smart

Sometimes, work means play. And when the occasional "off-campus" business event arises—a morale-boosting retreat with colleagues in Miami, a golf outing in Dubuque with potential clients—a whole new set of wardrobe challenges emerges. The mission: To fine-tune your wardrobe to accommodate casual work situations while still reflecting your professionalism and goals.

Entertainment

LOOKING YOUR BEST

Dark colors are slimming. From head to toe, monochromatic outfits create the illusion of height and deemphasize individual flaws or lack of proportion. Separates in different colors break up the body and highlight each area. Horizontal stripes emphasize the horizontal, making one look broader. Vertical stripes emphasize the vertical, visually elongating the body. Be sure to keep it simple in your problem area, wherever it may be; elaborate attempts to camouflage a body part will often call more attention to it.

SHOP SMART: EVENING

Wardrobe After Dark: Whether your job has you attending weekly black-tie extravaganzas or just the occasional office affair, you must always be prepared for a formal event. The goal is to put together one or more evening looks that are sleek, suitably dressy, in good taste, and not overtly sexy. In other words, clothes that say "polished" and

"professional," not "Party!" That means simple lines, classic shapes, high sophistication, and low exposure.

- Keep lines simple and classic—no prom dresses or ballooning ball skirts. Instead, choose straight or A-line styles.
- Details should be minimal. Flourishes like rhinestones and feathers are inappropriate in a business setting.
- Unless long, skirts should hang to or just below the knee.
- Hosiery should be sheer or semisheer.
- Shoes. Evening dress requires special shoes. Appropriate textures include peau de soie or a satin. A heel dresses things up but doesn't have to be high. (If unaccustomed to heels, avoid a height that makes you teeter.) And, as always with shoes, quality counts.
- Handbag. The smaller, the dressier. Styles include a wrist pouch, a clutch, or a structured, handled bag. Textures include silk and satin, occasionally embroidered or beaded. Avoid overcramming. Only bring

evening essentials: cash, lipstick, keys.

- Items that are simple and versatile. Buying individual pieces allows you to build an evening wardrobe that combines to create a handful of different looks.

1. Black pants. Pair with a beaded sweater set, a silk or satin blouse, or a bateau-neck knit. Add a dressy belt, heels, a small bag, and jewelry.
2. Long black skirt. Pair with unstructured top, knit top, dressy shoes, and jewelry.
3. Other options: A knee-length skirt, a silk shirt dress, a black shift dress.

HOW TO UPDATE YOUR DRESSY CLOTHES

If you've built a wardrobe you love, it can be a sad moment when some of your favorite pieces no longer fit or look fresh. Sometimes they can be salvaged. Pull out your dressy clothes and try each one on. If it's a little tight, perhaps the seams can be let out—ask a tailor. Usually, quality clothes have enough fabric built into the seams to be let out. If you haven't worn it for a while, consider revamping the look by altering the length or removing shoulder pads. A decorative jacket or an embroidered scarf can add color, texture, and sparkle while also changing the neckline. If you need something new, invest in a dress with simple lines, in an elegant fabric, which can easily be transformed by accessories.

WHY BLACK?

Black is simple, classic, elegant. It is always appropriate. It can provide all-out dazzle or anonymity. A black item can be worn over and over again and, with a quick switch of accessories, no one will be the wiser. Whether spiced up with a splash of color, a jolt of jewelry, or a shock of sparkle, black provides the right backdrop for the business at hand.

HOW TO BUY THE RIGHT BLACK PANTS

Just as every woman needs a good black dress, every woman needs the perfect pair of black pants. Unfortunately, one woman's perfect pants are another woman's nightmare. Pants hug the figure more than dresses or skirts. They can highlight waists, hips, thighs, even calves and ankles, but there are pants for nearly every figure type. It just may take a lot of trying on until you find the style that suits you.

If you have a "bubble butt"—one that protrudes roundly in the rear—look for pants that sit on the hips. Lines and details should be simple, with the rear pockets on jeans not so tiny. Flat derrières can benefit, however, from pocket detailing such as embroidery or flaps, but stay away from tight pants. Wide behinds or large thighs look better with pants that are bigger in the waist and have untapered legs. If you have narrow ankles, look for pants that taper at the ankle and are cut shorter, like Capri pants. Disguise hips and thighs with oversized, elongated tops. Wearing one color from neck to ankle also creates an illusion of height rather than width. Women with protruding stomachs may find pants with elastic waists more comfortable, but try to avoid extra fabric around the waist and hips. Wear tops made to be worn outside waistbands.

If you believe finding the right pair of pants is a mission impossible, work with a personal shopper. She has a wealth of experience and may be able to offer you something you hadn't considered. If you do find a style that suits you, buy extras or have more made in other fabrics. Your dressmaker or tailor will cut a pattern for you, and although it will cost extra, you will have the convenience of knowing you can have pants made each season that look great on you. Remember that fabrics of differing weights can fit differently. Larger, heavier women often look best in pants of lightweight fabric, while the thinnest women look best in pants made of substantial fabrics.

When choosing pants, try not to buy fabrics that wrinkle easily, but do look for fabrics that include stretch fibers. Even plus sizes benefit from the addition of up to 5 percent Lycra fibers. Those who previously found jeans uncomfortable now find they are living in stretch jeans.

When choosing black pants, it is especially important to find fabrics that will wear well and not become shiny. Velvets, corduroys, and faille are several of the fabrics that lose their luster over time. Wool gabardine or other lightweight wools are the best choices.

DRESSING ROOM CHECK

Use a three-way mirror. If you see a panty line, invest in a thong or sheer panties. If possible, try pants on with the shoes you'll wear with them. Some slim pants can be worn short, but most trousers need to break softly on the top of your shoes. If pants are too short, let down cuffs. If you are short, remove cuffs altogether—the longer line extends the leg. Avoid pants that tug across the stomach or thighs; try a cut with pleats, a fuller leg, or fabric that drapes. If a waistband is causing a tummy overhang, look for a lower-cut or higher-cut waist.

FIRST AID

Evening clothes often require special care due to special detailing or fabric. **Deciphering care labels:** A manufacturer or importer is only required to list one method of safe care, even if other safe methods exist. If a garment has a care label with washing instructions, it may or may not be dry-cleanable. There is no way to tell from the label. Some labels do inform consumers of all satisfactory care methods, but they do so on the volition of the manufacturer. If a garment is marked "Dry Clean," as opposed to "Dry Clean Only," and the fabric is constructed simply, you may have the option of laundering it, after you have tested for colorfastness. **Washing wools:** Chlorine bleach will damage wool fibers. Wash in Woolite. Roll in a towel to dry, then block and dry on a flat surface away from direct heat or sunlight. Steaming woolens can refresh them. **Cleaning cashmere:** Woven cashmere should be dry-cleaned, even if it is not tagged "Dry Clean Only." It may shrink if washed and dyes may run and become blotchy. If it is tagged to indicate that it can also be handwashed, block it flat to dry so it doesn't lose its form. Knit cashmere can be handwashed unless otherwise indicated. **Cleaning silk:** Silk scarves should be dry-cleaned. If washed, the consistency of a silk scarf may be altered depending on the finishing treatment used to give it sheen. Colors may run. Chlorine bleach damages silk and causes it to yellow.

Washable silk: Pre-wash treatments have made more silks washable. Silks that are often safe to wash include raw silk, China silk, India silk, crepe de chine, pongee, shantung, tussah, douppioni, and jacquard. Roll-dry in a towel to absorb moisture, then hang on a padded hanger. Machine drying silk will cause it to disintegrate. Instead, iron it on a low setting while slightly damp. **Care of velvet:** Never iron nylon velvets. Hang velvet on padded hangers; don't fold it. Dry-clean rayon velvet and acetate/rayon velvets. Frequent steaming and brushing with a soft brush can keep velvet fresh between wearings. Steaming helps fluff pile that has been crushed.

COMMUNICATING WITH YOUR DRY CLEANER

To assist in the professional removal of stains, take a stained garment promptly to the dry cleaner, and tell them what caused the stain. Areas damaged by attempts at home removal of stains can sometimes be corrected. **Sequins and beads:** If sequins or beads are glued onto a scarf, it should be dry-cleaned. A net should be used in dry-cleaning and the garment should be tested to ensure that beads don't come loose or that bead color doesn't run. If the sequins or beads are sewn onto a washable fabric, it can be handwashed in cool water and Woolite. **Dry-cleaning metallics:** It's risky to clean fabrics with metallic thread in them. They should be cleaned with petroleum or fluorocarbons instead of standard dry-cleaning fluid. **Removing stains by hand:** Success in stain removal, professionally or at home, is determined by the degree to which dyes and sizings (the finish applied to

fabric in manufacture) are colorfast when wet. Do not try to remove a stain yourself if the care label says "Dry Clean Only," if the garment is not colorfast, or if the stain is greasy. Because dyes and sizings tend to discolor with moisture, attempting to remove stains with water is not recommended without first testing the garment for colorfastness. Removal of a concentrated food or beverage stain is difficult. Try to absorb stains before they set by using the tip of a white paper towel to soak up excess liquid. Never scrub or press; it could ruin fabric texture.

Stains from toiletries, perfumes, and alcohol: Perfumes, hairspray, and toiletries contain alcohol, which can cause some dyes on silk to bleed or change color. Allow these products to dry on the body before you dress. Remove stains from alcoholic beverages as soon as possible. Some silk dyes, especially those in blue and green, are sensitive to alkalies, found in facial soaps, shampoos, detergents, and toothpastes. If color loss results from contact with these products, bring the scarf to your dry cleaner to discuss restoration. **Red wine or colored liquids:** Apply absorbent powder or salt, brush away, soak with mineral water or cool water; rinse with rubbing alcohol.

And on the opposite end of the spectrum…

SHOP SMART: BATHING SUITS

When bathing-suit season strikes again, you'd better act quickly or you'll be stuck wearing last year's number. If you enjoyed it then, it's likely to be a bit faded or stretched now—in other words, not guaranteed to look good for another summer. It's a cruel truth that the item we most hate to shop for is one that needs frequent replacing. But now for the good news: Though we can all point to the flaws in our figures, somewhere lies the perfect suit, designed to help us look our most beautiful. Fabrics like Lycra firm and lift; sheer panels reveal as they conceal; colors and pattern direct the eye toward one's best features and away from the worst. So relax—there's hope!

- Wear underwear that won't get in the way of bathing-suit lines.
- Allow time to try on lots of styles.
- Don't let suit sizes scare you—they're often labeled a size larger than your dress size.
- Bend, stretch, sit—does it move comfortably? Is the lining sufficient?
- And think lifestyle: Are you buying a suit for soaking in a hot tub (constant heat ruins fabrics, so don't spend too much) or soaking up the rays (a bandeau top minimizes tan lines), swimming laps (a tank is best).

HOW TO LOOK YOUR BEST IN A BATHING SUIT

Minimize the negative and accentuate the positive.

- No waist? Try a belted suit or a high-waisted two-piece.
- Small bust? Look for fabrics with body (velvet, crochet), details across the bust (ruffles), tops that push up and pad.
- Big bust? Wide straps and high necklines offer support.
- Heavy thighs? Avoid a high-cut leg; emphasize shoulders, bust, waist.
- Big bottom? Try a bottom with an inverted-triangle design, so the sides ease slightly up and out.

- Thick middle? Look for a princess bustline.
- Pear shape? Go for bright colors on top, dark on bottom.

TIPS FOR EVERYONE

What do most women want from a bathing suit? They want comfort. Comfort in the way it moves, what it reveals, and what it hides. If we fall out of our bathing suit when reaching, it doesn't work. If it rides up when walking, we're aggravated.

Next, women want a bathing suit to help their bodies look their best. Elongate the leg with a high cut, emphasize the back with something low and daring, or strut in a bikini if it shows a body off at its best.

The best thing you can wear with a bathing suit is sunglasses, sunblock, and a smile.

Sometimes we are called to dress up, even when bathing suits are required. Cover-ups can add elegance, accessories add flair, and swimsuits in unusual fabrics or attention-getting patterns add just the right amount of gaiety.

Bottom-heavy: Your best suit has a darker bottom than top, or a high neckline that broadens the shoulders, thereby balancing the figure. A bottom that is cut wider than about two inches at the side seam is a flattering proportion. For a big butt, the back of the suit should look like an inverted triangle, which will cup the curve of your entire rear by grabbing it at the center and letting go of it gradually as it extends to the sides.

No Waist: Look for belted suits, high-waisted two-pieces, and color-blocked full pieces with darker midriffs.

Round: Go for a suit in a darker color with princess seams or vertical stripes. Also look for high-tech fabrics like microfiber to hold you in!

Too Thin: Whites and pastel colors add weight; boy-leg silhouettes, horizontal stripes, and prints are also flattering. Look for suits with padded bras or a bust-enhancement feature. You want a feminine style that doesn't convey "cute."

Big Bust: Support from above and below will flatter a large bustline. Wide shoulders, thick straps, and empire waists with darts or shirring beneath the bust are ideal features. Some suits have "hidden" inner support like floating underwires or shelf bras. A deep V-neck with a slightly higher-cut armhole is an option for support and to compliment a large bustline.

Small Bust: Fabrics with built-in body like velvet, textured lace, and crochet add oomph. Prints, subtle details, and seaming across the bust all make the most of a small bustline.

Thick Middle: Curvy cut-outs and asymmetrical silhouettes are a flattering way to show your shape. Princess seams that trace the curve of the bust and waist minimize a thick middle.

Pot Belly: A brief that rests just below your belly button lends a subtle curve that accentuates the body rather than cutting it in half at the waist (look at the way lingerie briefs are cut by European manufacturers).

Pear Shape: Accentuate your shoulders with something asymmetrical or strapless. A cropped top with a boat neck will accentuate your collarbone. Pair this with a bikini cut so the legline reaches just below your hip bone. Avoid a high-cut suit.

From Sales Conference

When attending to business looking laid-back (whether at a sales conference or office retreat), crisp, clean casual wear fits the bill.

SMART OPTIONS

TOPS
Avoid anything extremely busy, excessive, or tight.

KNITS
- Shirts
- Quality tees

BOTTOMS
- Khakis
- Slacks
- Relaxed skirt (longer and softer is fine)

SHOES
- Comfortable flats
- Sandals

HOSIERY
If it's a casual venue in a warm place and your legs look good, bare legs should be fine.

to Retreat

A knit top has the slouch of a T-shirt with a touch of tailoring to keep it respectable.

SWEATER SET
Feminine and
pulled together.

V-NECK
Preppy, casual.
Can be layered
over a tee or
shell.

POLO SHIRT
Sporty spirit.
Most professional
when tucked in.

A.M.

From Drinks...

When dressing for evening in a relaxed business environment, opt for sleek and sophisticated—not sexy.

CASUAL CHIC DETAILS

Boat neck.

Fun necklace.

Three-quarter sleeves.

Color.

Small bag.

Silk shantung.

Casual sandals.

Sandals (higher heel is dressier).

to Dinner

Choose a decorative sweater instead of a plain cardigan and pair it with a camisole for a dressier look. Three-quarter sleeves allow you to get away with wearing a sweater in warmer climates. Black pants can take you from morning meeting to hospitality suite.

P.M.

Competitive Edge

Casual business outings can be clannish affairs, resulting in either a bonding experience or an alienating one. Clothes must be considered carefully. The teeny bikini you wear to bask on the beach with friends is likely to send an undesirable message when in the company of colleagues.

GOLF & TENNIS

Traditionally, professional women golfers were expected to follow the dress dictates of their male counterparts. Recently the possibilities for fashionable choices on the green have grown. Most private clubs do have guidelines for women golfers, and you should play it safe by checking in advance. Generally, it is better to wear knee-length shorts or skirts, but if this is too stifling, be sure that any hem rests no higher than four inches above the knee. Stay away from anything resembling a tank top. Shirts should have collars and sleeves. Not only does this provide better protection from the sun, but it also insures that you will be appropriately fashionable for the golf course.

White clothing and a collared shirt are still required at many venues. When in doubt, err on the side of caution. Clean tennis shoes, appropriate socks, and a hat are also advisable.

CAN YOU LOOK PROFESSIONAL IN A SWIMSUIT?

THE ANSWER IS YES

Business events near bodies of water present their own set of complications. The dress code is business casual, with the added challenge of dressing for "fun in the sun."

DRESS CODE

1. A one-piece bathing suit or tankini shows an appropriate level of modesty.
2. Except when swimming or sunbathing, wear a cover-up. Options: Sarong, long white shirt, cotton sweater, pull-on shorts, or skirt.

AVOID

1. A thong or bikini bathing suit.
2. A plunging neckline.
3. Anything sheer.

CEO =
COVERING
EVERYTHING
OBJECTIONABLE

Business Entertaining

Being a whiz at the board meeting—and then equally scintillating later, at the boss's son's bar mitzvah—is called serious multitasking. When building an evening wardrobe, you want clothes that are as multitalented and versatile as you are. Classic evening looks—from black stilettos to a satin-trimmed tuxedo—are always reliable and forever flexible.

WHAT A HEEL
Satin, velvet, and silk faille heels are appropriate for evening.

PERENNIAL BLACK
Year-round, black is an evening basic, no matter what color the outfit is.

EVENING EXTRAS
A structured black clutch, black gloves, and even red lipstick are timeless accessories suitable to a variety of after-dark events.

Right from Work...

If that five o'clock meeting is going to spill straight into an after-hours business affair, slip a shimmery top under your suit—your workaday suit will take on an evening sheen.

Keep a few key items stashed in your office and turning a day look into an evening one becomes a snap: A dressed-up top, evening heels, sheer hose, a festive handbag, a little makeup, and a subtle fragrance.

or Going Home First?

If you have the luxury of going home before your work function, be prepared. Have a simple black dress pressed and ready with appropriate accessories. What's appropriate? When business is conducted over cosmopolitans and current events— in other words, a cocktail party—dressing smart means clothes that are festive but not flashy.

COCKTAIL DRESS
The black cocktail dress is sleek, sophisticated, and classic. A simple, structured style dressed up with special accessories—sheer hosiery, either black or nude, with evening pumps, and a small evening bag. Pearls add a classic splash to any day or night look.

Black Tie

Galas, charity events, and award ceremonies have a special dress code unto themselves. A classic tuxedo is sophisticated, sexy, and original. With sharp satin lapels and pristine pant stripes, a tuxedo has the pomp and polish of menswear—with a dose of feminine flair. Make sure fit is impeccable. Pair the tailored pieces with festive, feminine details—a colorful, luxurious camisole; closed-toe stilettos with an evening sheen.

LE SMOKING
The Algerian-born Parisian designer Yves Saint Laurent took over the house of Dior at age 21 and branched out on his own at 25, at every step forging new ground in women's fashion and women's lives. Along with the pantsuit, he served up "Le Smoking," a square-shouldered take on the tuxedo jacket—heretofore strictly male domain—offering women independence, and confidence along with style.

A Formal Affair

A formal evening suit is simple, stunning, and for the many evening-phobes in our midst, safe. Whether the event is an industry benefit or a night at the opera with a key account, a black, floor-length gown and matching jacket are utterly elegant. Make sure the jacket is tailored to a T and the length of the dress suits the height of the heel you will wear.

Reality Check

"When women kiss it always reminds one of prize-fighters shaking hands."

H. L. MENCKEN

Whether you're seeking the perfect interview suit or making the jump to power player, having an overall fashion strategy is only half the picture. The difference is in the details, and here, we highlight the most critical ones: the good, the bad, the ugly (the ill-fitting, the embarassing...).

INTERVIEW WARDROBE
- Do you feel confident when you put on your suit?
- Do you feel comfortable when you sit in your suit? Does your skirt ride too high? Is there a gap between your socks and the hem of your pants?
- Are your shoes polished and in good shape?
- Are your undergarments visible at all?
- Can you see through your skirt in the light?
- Check your hosiery for runs and snags.
- Is your hair neat and tidy?
- Do you have excess facial hair? Wax, bleach, or remove with electrolysis.
- Are your nails fairly short, manicured, and subtly polished?
- Is your makeup natural, but flattering?
- Smile. Any food stuck between teeth?
- Does your jewelry make noise or attract attention?
- Is your purse organized so you are not rummaging through it during your interview?

- If you question what is appropriate dress, call the human resources person in advance for guidelines and err on the conservative side.
- Are you visually presenting the image you want to?

WORK WARDROBE
- Mirror check: Where does your eye fall first? If it doesn't go to your face, reconsider what you are wearing.
- Are you sending too many visual messages? Choose a colorful jacket, a decorative scarf, or a printed top and keep the rest of your outfit neutral.
- Check your shoes. Worn ones can bring down your look.
- Are you carrying too much? Does your bag look overwhelming?
- Does your hosiery unify your look or stand out?
- Check your nails. Poor grooming or chipped nail polish will ruin any look, no matter how expensive your clothing is.
- Can your wardrobe accommodate any work occasion?
- Are you dressing for the job you want?
- Does your outfit look like it's wearing you, or are you wearing it?
- Did you dress smart today?

POWER WARDROBE
- Fine, you can afford logos. But are they speaking louder than you?
- Do your clothes reflect a consistent personal yet professional style (in color, cut, attitude)?
- Are you dressing with authority?
- Are you comfortable in your clothes? Do they communicate the message you intend?
- Do you look successful, and confident?

TRAVEL AND ENTERTAINMENT
- Does your luggage look professional? Can you navigate it through an airport with ease? Can you find it easily at baggage claim?
- Do the clothes you wear to occasions outside the office reflect the professional image you desire?
- Are you comfortable when traveling?
- Is the sportswear you wear to professional outings in good shape, coordinated, and devoid of college or advertising slogans?
- Do you have the proper outerwear for evening clothes?

Dress Smart—A Lifetime Commitment

A closet overhaul isn't merely about skirt styles, heel heights, and the suit that will give you that extra oomph. America, unlike any other nation except possibly Australia, is the land of reinvention. And this book is a guide to that end—a how-to of self-discovery. The American philosopher William James said, in essence: Think differently, live differently. We say: Shop differently, live differently. Look at your closet in a new way, and you will necessarily look at yourself in a new way—and your life and circumstances will follow suit.

After all, what is a career if not a series of self-reinvention and personal developments? The leap from assistant to associate, or from manager to director, demands an expanded notion of yourself, your confidence, and your capabilities. Your wardrobe should be equally organic. Dressing Smart isn't just an exercise to haul out for a sudden job interview or a pending promotion—it's a nonstop evolution process, and a personal token of your dedication to, and investment in, yourself, your career, and your goals. It's a way of life.

The main message: You can shop your way to success—to a certain extent. But do so responsibly. Shop smart. Shop with a friend or work with a professional shopper. Shop regularly. Dressing smart is a lifetime commitment. There is no morning where it isn't important to look your best—you never know who will be riding to the 17th floor with you, munching airplane peanuts in seat 19C next to you, or showing up as a client who, it turns out, has the potential to open doors for you.

The easiest way to keep the focus and awareness necessary to have a high-functioning, career-boosting closet? The Chic Simple Process: Scheduled—perhaps seasonal—appointments between you and your wardrobe where you Assess (your goals, your clothes), DeJunk (old philosophies, stale styles), and ReNew (your motivations and the tools that will help you fulfill them).

In the (much-touted) world of impressions, you are what you wear. In business, your clothes often are perceived as a thumbnail sketch of your status and capability. By tapping into the thoughts on these pages, you will learn to take control of the image that you project in the workplace. The result is that your clothes will measure up to, and reflect, your ability—and you can forget about them, which is the ultimate goal. Then the only job you'll have to perform is the one you were hired to do.

RESOURCES

QUOTES

P 6 John Molloy, *The New Dress for Success* (Warner, 1988)
P 14 John Gray, *Mars and Venus in the Workplace* (HarperCollins, 2001)
P 17 Tina Brown, *The Wall Street Journal* (July 26, 2001)
P 18 Cathy Newman, *National Geographic Fashion* (Simon & Schuster, 2001) from *The New York Times*, (January 31, 2002)
P 24 Gloria Steinem, from *Women's Wicked Wit*, Michelle Lovric (Chicago Review Press, 2001)
P 31 Dwight D. Eisenhower, from *The Quotable Executive*, John Woods (McGraw-Hill, 2000)
P 38 Roger Ailes, *You Are the Message* (Irwin Professional Publishers, 1987)
P 62 Linda Ellerbee, *Move On* (1991) from *The New Beacon Book of Quotations by Women*, Rosalie Maggio (Beacon press, 1996)
P 64 Jane Friedman as interviewed by Kristy Zimbalist
P 68 Bill Blass, from *Fashion: Great Designers Talking*, Anna Harvey (MQ Publications Limited, 1998)
P 76 Diana Ross, from *The Great Rock 'N' Roll Quote Book*, Ed. Merrit Malloy (St. Martin's Griffin, 1995)
P 121 Ben Cheever, *Fast Company* (April 2002)
P 123 Robin Fisher Koffer, *Make a Name for Yourself* (Broadway Books, 2000)
P 128 Leo Tolstoy, from *The Artist's Way at Work: Riding the Dragon*, Mark Bryan with Julia Cameron and Catherine Allen (William Morrow, 1998)
P 130 Jerry Rubin, *Growing Up at Thirty-Seven* (M. Evans & Co., 1976)
P 164 N. F. Simpson, from *The Art of Looking Sideways*, Alan Fletcher (Phaidon Press Limited, 2001)
P 172 Anne Morrow Lindbergh, *Hour of Gold, Hour of Lead*, (Harcourt Press, 1973)
P 182 James Branch Cabell, *Something About Eve*, 1927, from *The New York Public Library Book of 20th Century American Quotations*, Ed. Stephen Donadio, Joan Smith, Susan Mesner, Rebecca Davidson (Warner, 1992)
P 200 H.L. Mencken, "Sententiae," *The Vintage Mencken*, 1955, from *The New York Public Library Book of 20th Century American Quotations*, Ed. Stephen Donadio, Joan Smith, Susan Mesner, Rebecca Davidson (Warner, 1992)
P 208 Michael Korda, *Power! How to Get it, How to Use it* (Random House, 1975)

PHOTOGRAPHY BY DAVID BASHAW EXCEPT:
James Wojick: 12 shoe, 15 suit, 22 suit, 23 TOP and BOTTOM
suit, 32 shirt, 36 makeup, 37 notepad group, 63 hosiery, 66
suit, 69 bracelets, 70 buttons, 92 sweater set, 106 belts, 107
suit with scarf, 118 two bags, 119 agenda, 120 outfit, 122 bag
group, 125 charm bracelet, 127 outfit, 149 clutches, 162 luggage, 165 toiletry, 179 dress, 181 qtips, 194-195 evening
Dana Gallagher: 6 pencil, 25 bank **Robert Tardio:** 173 leather
vest 152 outfit **Kenji Toma:** 16 tattoo; 176 luggage; 178 suit
ILLUSTRATIONS Eric Hanson: globe **Ruth Ansel:** Kim
and jeff

DEDICATION

With love to my children, Glenna and Carolyn, who make my
world rich and big, to my very chic simple mother, Evelyn
Johnson, and to my sisters, Susan Banta and Jill Johnson,
who live life with adventure and style—Kim

To Chuck, Robin and Jessica for the years of sharing family
and especially Chuck for the grace of helping during the
difficult times with always a smile and forgiveness—Jeff

ACKNOWLEDGMENTS

Lord & Taylor, Brooks Brothers, Talbots, Ralph Lauren,
Nordstrom, Banana Republic, John Molloy—*Dress for
Success*; Caterine Milinaire—*Cheap Chic*

INVALUABLE RESOURCES

Caryn Karmatz Rudy, Molly Chehak, Binky Urban, Ruth Ansel,
Mitchell Rosenbaum, Seth Bogner, Ali, Eugenia Fickens,
Henry at Union Square Cafe, Steve at Michaels, Jim Winters

CHIC SIMPLE STAFF

Partners Kim & Jeff
President Jim Winters
Style Consultant Laurie Bliss
Associate Style Editor Samantha Schoengold
Assistant Style Editor Marika Horacek
Production Director Andrea Weinreb
Office Manager Doug Moe

COMMUNICATIONS

Hi, good to be talking book talk again. It's been a couple of
years since our last Chic Simple book. We weren't on vaca-
tion, just growing the company. But as we said in the opening letter, we felt there was a need to address the changing
landscape of dressing in today's current workplace, and
books still work best. We still have our web site up,
www.chicsimple.com, which we get annoyed at because it is
always lagging behind what we are doing—the Internet is
like a public in-box of things constantly needing attention. It's
good hearing from all of you, even the woman from Paris
who came up to us as we were eating fish tacos at Club
Havana (it's just hard to talk with your mouth full). And it made
us so happy to hear from Remo the other day; let's hear it for
Australia. The big news is we moved out of the SoHo loft to an
office overlooking Union Square. There is something very special in being suspended over trees in New York City. As usual
you can write or e-mail or fax us at the office:

Chic Simple
200 Park Avenue South
New York, New York 10003
Fax: 212-473-0204
www.chicsimple.com

A NOTE ON THE TYPE

Why do we even comment on the type we use? Well, we
like type and with the advent of computers everyone has
tried his or her hand on the use of fonts and playing with
size and styles. Who hasn't blown up type or played
with **bold** and *italic*? Chic Simple has always tried to use
type as an element of design and also entertainment—
which occasionally appears to annoy people. For many
books we used New Baskerville (a serif typeface) for what is
called the body copy, and for captions and factoids the typeface Futura (sans serif) was utilized. The body copy of tho
two new Chic Simple titles is set in Minion while the captions and image guide information is in a sans-serif called
Helvetica Neue. **MINION** was created by Robert Slimbach;
it's a classical and very readable type we feel makes you
feel like you are with an old friend, which is what a book
should be about. What's nice about it is its aesthetic—a
page looks pretty and somehow elegant wearing it—while
it's still readable, a nice functional quality in a typeface.
Helvetica is the type of "the NEW" and like all things of the
"new" it was createded in the 60s. It was developed in
1961 by the German foundry D. Stempel AG and was originally named "Neue Haas Grotesk." We guess someone in
the marketing department mentioned that to have your customers constantly refering to your product as grotesque
might not be a brilliant move, so the name Helvetica came
into being. Smart move: Helvetica has become the most
popular typeface in the world. The version used in the two
new books is called **HELVETICA NEUE**, which is a redrawn
version of Helvetica with better uniformity between the different weights. Essentially it means that the different sizes
and bold appearances are more balanced. We're sure this is
way more information than you could possibly desire, but
have you ever known us not to beat a subject to death?

SEPARATION AND FILM BY

Butler & Tanner Limited
Frome, England

PRINTED AND BOUND BY

Butler & Tanner Limited
Frome, England

HARDWARE

It used to be fun to walk around the office as Chic Simple
was growing and list all the cool equipment that was being
used to create the books. The first books were done with
state-of-the-art Apple Macintosh Quad 700's. Ah, those
were the days. Remember how if the files were too big
instead of a photo that awful message would come up in a
field of gray, NOT ENOUGH MEMORY? And for accessing the
Internet there was a noble Supra Modem: Download time
was measured in days. Today it's just overwhelming: We
have old rugged stealth Macintosh G-3's, fancy Macintosh
G-4's with attitude, iMacs running around the halls misbe-
having, and the occasional slightly disapproving PC. There
are hubs, networks, scanners, and a growing battery of
printers whose sole purpose is to sit around in the afternoon
and swig toner. Everyone seems to be IM-ing online and we
still don't understand what happened between T-1 and T-3
lines, did we just miss T-2? Also, where does old equip
ment go? It seems to just disappear. Is it like elephants?
Is there somewhere near Santa Cruz or San Jose a field full
of old Syquest drives in retirement? Anyway, most of our
storage is devoted to MP-3s which is a segue into...

MUSICWARE

Wilco *(Summerteeth)*, Morphine *(Good)*, St. Germain
(Tourist), Air *(Moon Safari)*, Michael Bloomfield *(Don't Say
That I Ain't Your Man)*, Eric Clapton & B.B. King *(Riding with
the King)*, Van Morrison *(Philosopher's Stone)*, Arturo
Delmon/Nathaniel Rosen *(Music for a Glass Bead Game)*,
Philp Glass *(Dancepieces)*, Sir Neville Marriner *(Mozart Wind
Concerti)*, Lucinda Williams *(Essence)*, The Roches *(Zero
Church)*, Various Artists *(WFUV-City Folk Live)*, Ja Rule *(Pain
Is Love)*, Various Artists *(Le Flow)*, Various Artists *(Jackson
Pollock Jazz)*, Charles Lloyd *(Voices in the Night)*, Charlie
Haden *(Nocturne)*, Chet Baker *(Sentimental in Paris)*, Django
Reinhart & Stephane Grappelli *(Swing from Paris)*, Louis
Armstrong *(Hot Fives & Sevens)*, Oscar Peterson *(Plays
Count Basie)*, Roy Hargrove *(Moment to Moment)*, Sarah
Vaughan *(The Complete Mercury)*, Badly Drawn Boy *(The
Hour of Bewilderbeast)*, Bruce Springsteen *(Bootleg
Philadelphia Concert*—Thank you George*)*, U2 *(Beautiful
Day)*, Harmonia Ensemble *(Fellini-L'Uomo del Sogni)*, Anne
Sofie von Otter & Elvis Costello *(For the Stars)*, Frank Sinatra
(Songs for Swinging Lovers), Paolo Conte *(The Best of)*, Tom
Waits *(Beautiful Maladies)*, Bob Marley *(Songs of Freedom-
Disc 4)*, Mercedes Sosa *(30 Años)*, Omara Portuondo *(Omara
Portuondo)*, Charles Aznavour *(Greatest Golden Hits)*, June
Tabor *(Against the Streams)*, Bryan Ferry *(As Time Goes By)*,
Jussi Bjoerling *(The Pearl Fishers Duet)*, June Monheit
(Never Never Land), Van Morrison with George Fame &
Friends *(How Long Has This Been Going On)*, Wong Kar-wai
(In the Mood for Love), Bebel Gilberto *(Tanto Tempo)*, Cesaria
Evora *(Cafe Atlantico)*, Etta James *(Blue Gardenia)*, Joe
Henderson *(Lush Life)*, Bob Dylan *(Love and Theft)*, Leonard
Cohen *(Ten New Songs)*. None of the books could ever have
made it through the dark empty nights of flowing copy into
pages without the steadfast beacon of PIG radio (KPIG
to the uninitiated) beaming its message of a better world
through pick'n and sing'n from its golden home on the
shores of Freedom county to the dark twisted urban canyon
lands of our New York offices. Thank you, PIG.
jeff and Kim

CHIC
SIMPLE ™
library

"All life is a game of power. The object of the game is simple enough: to know what you want and get it."

MICHAEL KORDA
Power!